Golf Rules Explained

GOLF®
MAGAZINE
Golf Rules Explained

Edited by David Barrett

THE LYONS PRESS
Guilford, Connecticut
An imprint of The Globe Pequot Press

The Lyons Press is an imprint of The Globe Pequot Press.

10 9 8 7 6 5 4 3 2 1

Printed in the United States of America

Text design by Casey Shain

ISBN 1-58574-509-X

Library of Congress Cataloging-in-Publication Data is available on file.

Contents

● Chapter 3—Hazards

● Chapter 4—Out of Bounds/Lost Ball

● Chapter 5—On the Green

Chapter 6 — Ball Moved or Deflected

Chapter 7 — Dropping/Placing

Chapter 8 — Abnormal Ground Conditions

Introduction

Surveys of our readers at *GOLF MAGAZINE* show that articles on the Rules of Golf are among the most widely read pages in our publication. When we ask the readers what they'd like to see more of, the Rules rate close behind our bread-and-butter instructional articles. This paints a picture of a corps of golfers devoted to and knowledgeable about the Rules.

Hide behind a tree at any golf course, though, and you'll see a much different picture. The fact is, not many golfers adhere strictly to all of the Rules when they play. While this is certainly true of casual golfers, it is also to a large degree true of more serious players — including the subscribers who answer our surveys. For some reason, it seems that people enjoy reading about the Rules more than they do following them.

So, what's going on here? It's not that we're a nation of golf cheaters, is it? Sure, there are the occasional louts who try to get away with something while their opponents or fellow competitors aren't looking. But they're only a small part of the picture.

The truth is that most golfers just don't know the Rules very well. As is befitting a sport of so much age and austerity, the Rules of Golf are complicated, and their interpretations equally complex. The idea of schooling oneself in the minutiae of the Rules and their many variables is such an intimidating prospect that most golfers, even those on the professional tours, don't even try. The pros certainly deserve respect for their integrity in playing a game where there are no referees and in which they call penalties on themselves, but their Rules knowledge is sometimes lacking. Every year, there are numerous reports of instances in which players cost themselves strokes or were even disqualified for violating Rules they didn't know existed or which they didn't know well enough.

The typical golfer's Rules knowledge is even worse. We conducted a quiz on our web site, www.golfonline.com, asking five questions provided by the United States Golf Association, the game's Rule-making body (along with the Royal and Ancient Golf Club of St. Andrews, Scotland, which has jurisdiction overseas). Four questions were rated by the USGA as moderate in difficulty and the fifth was a stumper. The respondents got only 29 percent of the answers correct, a score not much better than they would have earned with random guessing in the multiple-choice format. This is telling.

There is also the sense that casual golf is a different affair than tournament golf. Serious golfers know it is a penalty to ask another player about club selection before playing a shot, but they probably wouldn't slap their buddy with a two-stroke penalty for doing so in a friendly round. This assertion is supported by a separate GOLFONLINE survey we conducted, in which only 23 percent of those polled said that they strictly follow every Rule in all the rounds they play.

We're left with two possible conclusions about why golfers like to read about the Rules, then. One is that they are aware that it is an area where they need to improve their knowledge, so they soak up Rules articles much in the same way they turn toward instructional tips to knock strokes off their game. Or, perhaps they just get a vicarious thrill from learning about the Rules, even if they don't plan on applying them to their own game.

The Rules themselves, however — far from being dry — can be a highly entertaining subject in their own right. We're not suggesting that they belong on your bookshelf alongside your Tom Clancy novels (though you should keep a copy of the Rules in your golf bag). But, in their application and inherent intricacy, the Rules can indeed become fascinating. All sorts of crazy things can happen on golf courses, and when they do, the Rules interpretations can be pretty crazy, too.

That's the basis for my monthly column in GOLF MAGAZINE called "Within the Rules," which forms the basis for this book. The guiding principle of the column is that the best way to learn the Rules is by using real golf situations as examples. Each column — and each selection in this book — contains two such situations, the first setting up the main premise and the second, with the heading "Now What If," offering up a different, often surprising, twist.

The richness of the Rules as a subject is illustrated by the fact that "Within the Rules" has been running since 1992, and there is still no shortage of topics to discuss. Some of the columns have been inspired by situations passed along by GOLF MAGAZINE readers, and many of the others were based on entries found in Decisions on the Rules of Golf (a joint publication of the USGA and R&A that gives official rulings on more than a thousand situations).

The hope is that the selected situations in this book will elicit the response, "Wow! I wouldn't have guessed that." The emphasis on entertainment value and the element of surprise have led to a number of selections involving unusual situations that might never happen to you (or anybody you know) on the golf course. But, in explaining the rulings for those situations, more common situations are illuminated as well. So, there's plenty of practical, useful information to be absorbed along the way.

The selections are grouped into 12 individual chapters. These involve areas of the golf course ("On the Tee" or "Hazards"), types of situations ("Ball Moved or Deflected"), or forms of play ("Match Play"). And there is also a handy, easy-to-reference index that will enable you to look up particular selections by Rule number.

By the time you finish reading *Golf Rules Explained*, it is my hope that you'll know all you'll ever need to about the Rules of Golf. How you use this knowledge—even *whether* you use it at all—is up to you.

David Barrett
May 2003

CHAPTER ONE

On the Tee

Out of Order

What happens when a player hits from the wrong tee?

Steve and Bill are playing a match on an unfamiliar course. After playing the second hole, they go to the nearby sixth tee instead of the third tee. Steve hits his drive, then Bill realizes they are on the wrong teeing ground. What is the procedure?

The provisions for playing from the wrong teeing ground are the same as for playing from outside the teeing ground on the correct hole (Rules 11-4 and 11-5). In match play, this leads to an interesting situation. Bill has the option of canceling Steve's stroke and having him play it again from the proper area. If Bill elects not to recall the stroke, Steve's ball is in play—on the third hole. He must make his way from the sixth fairway to the third green; meanwhile, Bill proceeds to the third tee and plays the hole normally.

Of course, Steve can always concede the hole rather than complete it by this roundabout route. But you can imagine his satisfaction if he were to halve or win the hole.

If they were competing in stroke play, Steve's ball would not be considered in play. He would be penalized two strokes and play from the third tee; the stroke he played from the wrong tee wouldn't count. In stroke play, the player can correct his error before playing from the next tee (in this case, the seventh); after that, he's disqualified.

Now What If?

Steve and Bill are playing a match on an unfamiliar course. They both hit shots from the sixth tee when they should be playing the third hole. They realize their mistake when they are in the sixth fairway. What is the procedure?

Steve and Bill disregard all play on the sixth hole, go to the third tee, and resume their match. Once both players hit from the wrong teeing ground, the provisions of Rule 11-4 no longer apply in match play. But they must play the holes in correct sequence, so even if they finish playing the wrong hole, the result of the hole doesn't count. They can correct the error at any time, even after playing several holes.

In the Way

Can a player move a tee marker to clear a path for his swing?

Terry decides to tee the ball on the extreme left of the teeing ground. He tees it legally within the teeing ground, then picks up the tee marker and moves it because it's in the way of his swing. After playing his shot, he replaces the tee marker. Is this allowed?

No. Before a player plays his first stroke from the teeing ground of the hole being played, the tee markers are deemed to be fixed (Rule 11-2). If he moves a tee marker to avoid interference with his stance, the area of his intended swing, or his line of play, he is penalized two strokes in stroke play or loss of hole in match play under Rule 13-2. There is no penalty if he replaces the tee marker before he, or anyone else in the group, plays a stroke.

In other circumstances where the player is not improving his stance, swing, or line of play, it is all right to move a tee marker. A player is not penalized for moving a tee marker by falling over it or by kicking or striking it with a club. He may even pick it up for no apparent reason. In all such cases, the tee marker should be replaced.

However, if a player moves a tee marker before or after playing from the teeing ground because he thinks the tee markers are too close together, aimed in the wrong direction, or for some other reason, he is disqualified unless the tee marker is replaced before he or anyone else plays from the teeing ground.

Now What If?

While playing the fifth hole, Terry's wild drive comes to rest on the third tee, near one of the tee markers. The tee marker interferes with his swing, so Terry moves it and then replaces it after the stroke. Is this allowed?

Yes. Tee markers are deemed to be fixed only before the first stroke on the hole being played. At any other time, they are movable obstructions and may be moved without penalty.

Not So Fast

What's the proper order for hitting a provisional ball?

Steve hits his tee shot deep into the woods, where the ball might be lost. He announces that he will play a provisional ball, and plays the provisional before his opponent in match play, Tom, hits his tee shot. Has Steve proceeded correctly?

No. When a player plays a provisional ball from the tee, he should do so after his opponent in match play—or fellow competitors in stroke play— have played their first strokes (Rule 10-3). If he doesn't wait for the others to hit before playing his provisional, he is guilty of playing out of turn.

In stroke play, Steve's mistake is unimportant because there is no penalty for playing out of turn unless it is done to give any player an advantage (Rule 10-2c). In match play, however, there are potential ramifications. The opponent may require a player who has played out of turn to cancel the stroke and play a ball in the proper order, without penalty (Rule 10-1c). However, the decision must be made immediately. Tom can't wait until after he hits his own tee shot to make the call on requiring Steve to replay.

Now What If?

In stroke play, Steve hits his tee shot too far on a par-three hole and his ball ends up in thick woods. He announces that he will play a provisional ball and says he will play the provisional before his fellow competitor, Tom, hits so that Tom can get a better idea about what club to hit. Tom agrees and watches Steve hit the provisional ball. Is there a penalty?

Yes, because Steve played out of turn in order to give Tom an advantage. Both players are disqualified. This ruling is made because the players agreed to play in the wrong order so that Tom could see what club Steve hit. If Steve played out of turn only to speed play or because he didn't know the right order, there is no penalty.

In Line for Trouble?

The Rules don't give you free rein in lining up your shots

As he tees up his ball, Jim notices a broken tee a couple of yards ahead of the markers. He tees up behind it so he can aim his tee shot over it. As he takes his stance, he sees that the broken tee isn't quite on a direct line with his target. He uses his driver to nudge the broken tee over a few inches so it rests directly in front of his ball, then hits the shot. Has Jim acted properly?

No. Jim is penalized two strokes in stroke play, or loss of hole in match play, for placing a mark to indicate the line of play and leaving it there during the stroke (Rule 8-2).

Jim's actions were legal until he moved the tee with his club. Many players like to use a spot a few yards in front of the ball as an alignment aid, be it a divot, a discolored patch of grass, a broken tee, or something else. In fact, this alignment tip was popularized by Jack Nicklaus. But you can't create your own mark; you must use something already there. When Jim noticed his line with the broken tee was slightly off, he should have reteed his ball instead of moving the broken tee.

A mark may be placed on the player's line so long as it is moved away before the stroke (except on the green, where placing such a mark is never allowed). A player also can have someone indicate the line of play by standing on it, as may be necessary on a blind shot over a hill, but the person must move off the line before the stroke is played.

Jim places a club on the ground to help him properly align his feet. He then tosses the club aside before hitting the shot. Is this allowed?

Yes. Because he removed the club before playing the stroke, there was no Rules violation. Had Jim left the club on the ground during the stroke, he would have broken the Rule on indicating the line of play and been penalized two strokes in stroke play, or loss of hole in match play.

Swing and a Miss

A whiff is bad enough—don't compound it with a penalty

Paul whiffs his tee shot, but the ball topples off the tee from the force of the swing. He picks up the ball, retees it, then plays again from the tee. What is the ruling?

In stroke play, Paul's second attempt from the tee is his fourth stroke—the initial whiff counts as a stroke and he is assessed two penalty strokes. In match play, he loses the hole.

When Paul swung and missed with his first stroke, the ball was in play (Rule 14) and he should have played it from where it came to rest on the ground. The penalty for lifting a ball in play is one stroke (Rule 18-2a). Had Paul realized his mistake at this point and replaced the ball, he would have been hitting three and would not have suffered a loss-of-hole penalty in match play.

But since he played his next stroke from the tee instead of replacing the ball, he incurs the general penalty for Rule 18—two strokes in stroke play or loss of hole in match play. In stroke play, the two-stroke penalty overrides the one-stroke penalty for lifting the ball so only a total of two strokes are assessed.

One other point to make about whiffed tee shots: If you miss the ball with your first swing, be careful not to accidentally knock the ball off the tee before your next stroke. Normally, this is not a penalty. But since the whiff counts as a stroke, the ball is now in play, and knocking it off the tee calls for a one-stroke penalty.

Now What If?

Paul whiffs his tee shot, and the ball stays on the tee. He pushes his tee farther into the ground and plays. What is the ruling?

Paul is penalized two strokes in stroke play or loss of hole in match play. The ball was in play after his whiff. A player is not allowed to move his ball in play, and by teeing it lower he has moved the ball downward. That's a one-stroke penalty. Then, for not subsequently replacing it, Paul is assessed the further penalty.

CHAPTER TWO
In the Fairway/Rough

Touchy Situation

Can a player touch or lift a ball to identify it as his?

Wayne hits his drive into heavy rough. He finds a ball where he thinks his came to rest, but not enough of the ball is visible for him to identify it as his. Is he allowed to lift the ball in order to identify it?

Yes, with certain specifications (Rule 12-2). In fact, he should do so, because if the ball isn't his and he hits it, he will be penalized for playing a wrong ball.

Before he lifts the ball, the player must announce his intention to his opponent in match play or his marker or fellow competitor in stroke play. He must mark the position of the ball and give his opponent, marker, or fellow competitor an opportunity to observe the lifting and replacement. He can clean the ball only to the extent necessary to identify it. If the ball is in fact his, he then replaces it, which means putting it back in the same lie as he found it (for example, he can't sit it on top of the grass if it was sitting down originally).

The penalty for violating these provisions is one stroke in either match play or stroke play, except that if he fails to replace the ball properly he is penalized two strokes in stroke play or loss of hole in match play (Rule 20-3a).

If Wayne's ball were in a hazard, he would not be allowed to lift it to identify it — nor would he be penalized if he played a wrong ball from the hazard.

Now What If?

Wayne's ball is half buried in the rough. After announcing his intention to his opponent, marker, or fellow competitor, he touches the ball and rotates it so he can see the markings. By doing so, he identifies the ball as his. Is he penalized?

Yes, one stroke for touching the ball other than as provided in the Rules. Even if he doesn't lift the ball, he still must mark it before he is allowed to touch it under Rule 12-2. If he had marked the ball, there would have been no penalty, assuming the rotating in the grass didn't result in cleaning the ball beyond the extent necessary to identify it.

Timber!

What happens when a player meets interference from a fallen tree?

Mark hits his drive into the woods. It comes to rest near a fallen tree, which interferes with his swing. The fallen tree is fairly heavy, but, with effort, it can be moved. Is Mark permitted to move the tree?

Yes, if it is no longer attached to the stump. In such a case, the fallen tree is a natural object which is not fixed or growing, and is thus considered a loose impediment (Rule 23). If the fallen tree is attached to the stump, however, it is not "loose," and therefore may not be moved.

Loose impediments of any size or weight may be moved, provided that in doing so the player does not unduly delay play. The player is allowed to get help from fellow competitors, caddies, or anyone else in moving a heavy object. He is also allowed to break off part of a large loose impediment (for example, a branch of a fallen tree interfering with his swing) rather than move the whole thing.

If, on the other hand, a tree stump interferes with a player's swing, he has no recourse. He can't move the stump because it's not loose, and he generally doesn't get relief from it. He only gets relief if the stump has been marked as ground under repair or is in the process of being unearthed or cut up for removal, in which case it is "material piled for removal" and thus automatically ground under repair.

Now What If?

A tree has fallen onto the fairway due to a windstorm. It is still attached to the stump, and therefore not a loose impediment. Can Mark get relief from the fallen tree as ground under repair?

Yes, but not on his own. The tree doesn't meet the definition of ground under repair, but the player can request relief from the committee. Decision 25/9 states that the committee would be justified in declaring the area covered by the tree to be ground under repair. If the tree has fallen into the woods instead of the fairway, however, the player shouldn't expect a favorable ruling.

Stuck in Jail

An ill-considered swing can lead to big trouble

Bob hits his tee shot into the woods, where it comes to rest in an area of dense underbrush. He barely moves the ball with his next stroke and decides to declare the ball unplayable. Dropping within two club-lengths won't leave him a better shot, nor will dropping on a line behind the point where the ball lay. Is he allowed to go back to the tee to play his next stroke with a one-stroke penalty?

No. Rule 28a allows a player who has declared a ball unplayable to play "a ball...at the spot from which the original ball was last played." The ball was last played from the trees, so going back to the tee is no longer an option.

You should think twice before hitting from an area that is mostly unplayable—if you fail to escape the jungle with your swing, you might have to take a number of penalty strokes to get out. If the option of dropping behind the point of the ball on a line extending from the hole only gets you deeper into trouble, the only option is to take a series of two-clublength drops, each with a one-stroke penalty, until you reach a playable spot.

If Bob goes back and plays from the tee, he is penalized for playing from the wrong place. In match play, he loses the hole. In stroke play, he is penalized two strokes and required to finish the hole from the right place (he is disqualified if he plays from the next tee without correcting the error).

Now What If?

Bob hits his tee shot into the woods and it comes to rest in an area of dense underbrush. He declares the ball unplayable, takes a drop, and his ball rolls into another unplayable lie. He declares the ball unplayable again. Is he allowed to go back to the tee for his next stroke?

Yes. He has not made a stroke at the ball since the tee shot, so the tee is the spot from which the ball was last played. The penalty is two strokes because he declared the ball unplayable twice.

Kicked Around

What's the ruling when a ball is moved during a search?

Tony's drive ends up in deep rough. He accidentally kicks the ball while searching for it in the long grass. Is he penalized?

Yes. Tony is penalized one stroke and he is required to replace the ball (Rule 18-2).

The penalty would also apply to Tony if his caddie or partner in a team match causes the ball to move. If anyone else moves the ball while searching for it, there is no penalty. In match play, a player is not penalized for moving an opponent's ball during a search, nor is there a penalty in stroke play for moving a fellow competitor's ball. Therefore, if anyone is to use a club or foot to root around in deep rough for a lost ball, it should be an opponent or fellow competitor. A few things to note:

Other than during a search, a player is penalized one stroke for moving or touching an opponent's ball; there is no penalty at any time for moving a fellow competitor's ball in stroke play.

A player is not penalized for accidentally touching his ball if the ball does not move (sinking into the grass counts as movement).

There are some exceptions where a player is not penalized for accidentally causing his ball to move, mostly to do with lifting, replacing, measuring, and removing a movable obstruction.

Now What If?

Tony's ball is so deeply buried in a bunker that it cannot be seen. He probes for it with his foot and moves the ball. Is he penalized?

No. When the ball is in a hazard (bunker or water hazard), there is no penalty for accidentally moving it during a search. The ball must be replaced and the lie restored, with only enough sand removed so that part of the ball is visible. There is also no penalty for moving a ball while searching for it in casual water or ground under repair.

Up a Tree

An imaginative way to dislodge a ball from a tree branch— but is it legal?

Frank's ball ends up lodged in a tree branch, beyond the reach of a club. Frank swings at a lower part of the branch with a club so that the movement of the branch dislodges the ball, which falls to the ground. Is this permitted?

No. A "stroke" is defined as the forward movement of the club made with the intention of fairly striking at and moving the ball (Rule 14). Frank did not strike at the ball, so he did not make a stroke, even though his intention was to move the ball. He incurs a one-stroke penalty for causing his ball in play to move (Rule 18-2a) and is required to replace the ball.

Since the spot where the ball lay is difficult to reach and impossible to swing at, the player would proceed under the unplayable ball Rule, taking an additional one-stroke penalty and dropping the ball within two club-lengths of the point on the ground directly below the place the ball lay in the tree (Rule 28).

Another thing to keep in mind if the ball is in a tree is that for the ball

to be declared unplayable, it must be identified as the player's, otherwise it is lost (Rule 27). If the ball is lodged in the tree and the player wishes to dislodge it by shaking the tree so he can identify the ball and declare it unplayable, he must state his intention beforehand. Otherwise, he is subject to a one-stroke penalty for causing the ball to move.

Now What If?

Frank's ball lies against a board at the base of an out-of-bounds fence. He swings a club from the out-of-bounds side of the fence, striking the board and causing the ball to move. Is this permitted?

Yes. Frank is considered to have struck "at" the ball, even though other material intervened between the club and the ball (Decision 14-1/5), because the swing path was directly toward the ball.

Root of the Problem

Is a player allowed to probe for roots?

Robert's tee shot comes to rest in a wooded area. A twig lies directly behind his ball, and Robert can't tell if the twig is loose or is attached to its roots. Robert pulls on the twig and discovers that it is attached, and, therefore, he is not allowed to move it. Is he penalized if, by pulling on the twig, he improved the area of his intended swing?

There is no penalty, provided he returns the twig to its original position before playing his next stroke.

He would appear to be in danger of breaking Rule 13-2, which states that a player is not allowed to improve the position or lie of his ball, the area of his intended swing, his line of play, or the area in which he intends to drop or place a ball by moving, bending, or breaking anything growing or fixed. But since he is allowed to move a loose impediment (a natural object not fixed or growing), the Rules' makers provide some leeway.

According to Decision 13-2/26, a player is allowed to move a natural object to determine whether it is loose provided it is returned to its original position before the next stroke, the key condition being that he has not improved his situation by his actions. If the object has become detached, or if it is impossible to restore its original position, the player is penalized two strokes in stroke play or loss of hole in match play.

Now What If?

Robert's tee shot comes to rest in a wooded area in a position where he believes tree roots might be just below the ground's surface. Is he allowed to probe the area around his ball with a tee to find out if his club would strike a root in the course of his stroke?

Yes, provided there is a reasonable possibility that there are roots in the area and that the lie of the ball, area of intended swing, or line of play isn't improved and the ball is not moved (Decision 13-2/27).

Divot Dilemma

Can a player move a replaced divot if it's in his way?

Tom's ball lies in the fairway, just in front of a replaced divot. The divot has been carelessly replaced and will interfere with Tom's backswing. Tom removes or presses down the divot before making his stroke. Is this allowed?

No. Tom is penalized two strokes in stroke play or loss of hole in match play. Rule 13-2 prohibits a player from improving the area of his intended swing by removing or pressing down replaced divots (or other cut turf placed in position, sand, loose soil, or other irregularities of surface), with certain exceptions that don't apply in this case.

Tom would be allowed to move an unreplaced divot, which is a loose impediment. A replaced divot, however, isn't considered loose. When is a divot considered to be replaced? When substantially all of it, with the roots downward, lies in the divot hole (if the divot is upside down, it's a loose impediment), even if the hole isn't the one from which the divot was extracted. A divot that is not completely detached is not a loose impediment, even if all of it does not lie in the divot hole, and may not be moved in order to clear the way for a swing.

Now What If?

Tom's ball lies on the fringe of the green, just in front of the pitch-mark the ball made when it landed. The pitch-mark interferes with Tom's backswing. Tom steps on the pitch-mark to flatten it. Is this allowed?

No. Tom is penalized two strokes in stroke play or loss of hole in match play for improving the area of his intended swing by pressing down irregularities of surface. He must wait until after taking his stroke to fix the pitch-mark. He would also be penalized if he fixed a pitch-mark off the green on his line of play. If the pitch-mark were made by a fellow competitor's ball after Tom's ball came to rest, Tom would be allowed to fix it before playing.

Sand Splash

Can a player brush away sand from his line on the fringe?

Steve's ball lies on the fringe of the green, a few feet off the putting surface. He plans to use his putter for his next stroke. There is some sand on the fringe from an explosion shot from a greenside bunker made by a player in a previous group. Steve brushes away some sand from the fringe on his line and plays his stroke. Is this allowed?

No. Under Rule 23, sand and loose soil are considered to be loose impediments only on the green. Steve is penalized two strokes in stroke play or loss of hole in match play for improving his line of play (Rule 13-2).

Loose impediments are natural objects such as stones, leaves, twigs, insects, and the like, provided they are not fixed or growing, are not solidly embedded in the ground, and do not adhere to the ball (Rule 23). Any of these can be removed without penalty, unless both the loose impediment and the ball lie in or touch the same hazard.

Sand and loose soil, however, are considered to be just part of the ground except on the specially manicured surface of the green. This doesn't extend to the fringe, even though players often use a putter from there.

Steve could have removed any part of the sand that had splashed onto the green, but not any from off the green.

Now What If?

Steve's ball lies on the fringe of the green. One of his fellow competitors, Jim, then plays a stroke from a greenside bunker and splashes sand onto the fringe in front of Steve's ball. Is Steve allowed to remove the sand?

Yes. Steve is entitled to the lie and line of play he had when his ball came to rest. He is allowed to remove the sand from his line of play, and can also lift and clean his ball if any sand landed on it.

Snap Decision

Breaking a branch could mean a penalty

Ted hits his tee shot into the woods. His ball rolls underneath a tree so branches interfere with his next stroke. Ted makes a practice swing to determine how far back he can take the club and, in doing so, his club breaks one of the branches. Is he penalized?

Yes. A player is not allowed to improve the area of his intended swing by bending or breaking anything growing or fixed (Rule 13-2). Ted is penalized two strokes in stroke play, loss of hole in match play. Intent doesn't matter: Breaking the branch with a practice swing has the same effect as breaking it with a hand, so the penalty is the same.

A player is allowed to bend or break branches in fairly taking his stance, but that's all. He can't move branches with his hands to get them out of the way of his swing, he can't stand on a branch to keep it from interfering, he can't even bend a branch that obscures his view of the ball. He can move branches with his body, but only to the extent necessary to take a stance. Any practice swings must leave the situation intact. He could even be penalized for knocking off leaves during a practice swing if it's determined the action improved the area of his swing.

If Ted breaks the branch during the swing itself, it's a different story. Breakage is allowed while making a stroke or during the backward movement for a stroke.

Now What If?

Ted's swing is restricted by branches of a tree. He breaks a branch on his backswing, and discontinues his swing before striking the ball. Is he penalized?

Yes. There would have been no penalty for breaking the branch during a stroke. In this case, however, there was no stroke because the player stopped his club before striking the ball. Therefore, it's a two-stroke penalty in stroke play, loss of hole in match play.

Cleaning Up

When is a player allowed to clean his ball?

Greg's ball lies on the fringe of the green. Without thinking, he picks up his ball and cleans it. He then realizes he has broken the Rules because the ball did not lie on the green. Is he penalized twice – once for lifting the ball and once for cleaning it?

No. Greg is penalized one stroke in stroke play or match play for lifting the ball (Rule 18-2), but he suffers no penalty for cleaning it. Rule 21 says a ball not on the green may not be cleaned when lifted under three specific Rules (a ball on the green may always be lifted and cleaned). This means that a ball may be cleaned when lifted under any other Rule, and also that it may be cleaned when it is lifted illegally.

The exceptions to being able to clean the ball when lifted are if the ball has been lifted to determine if it is unfit for play (Rule 5-3) for identification (Rule 12-2), or because it is interfering with or assisting play (Rule 22). If a player cleans his ball under any of these circumstances when his ball isn't on the green, he is penalized one stroke.

If a player's ball is not on the green, he is allowed to clean it of loose impediments (including a live insect) as long as he does so without lifting, moving, or purposely touching the ball, which would be a one-stroke penalty. However, anything adhering to the ball, such as mud, is not a loose impediment and can't be removed (Rule 23).

Now What If?

Greg's ball lies off the green. It has rolled through a recently mown area and is covered with cut grass. Is he allowed to remove the grass from the ball?

No. The cut grass is adhering to the ball and therefore does not meet the definition of loose impediments. Greg is penalized one stroke if he cleans the ball, even if he does so without lifting the ball.

CHAPTER THREE

Hazards

Hazardous Putting

What can you do when your putt finds a greenside hazard?

Bob has a downhill putt on a fast green, with the pin cut near the front of the green. He hits the ball too hard and watches in dismay as it rolls past the hole, off the green, and down a slope into a water hazard in front of the green. It is not a lateral water hazard, and the ball is not playable from the hazard. What are Bob's options?

Bob is not allowed to drop the ball on the green side of the water hazard at the point the ball entered because it is not a lateral hazard. A ball resting in a "regular" water hazard must be dropped behind the hazard, regardless of which side of the hazard the ball entered (Rule 26-1). Bob can drop a ball, with a one-stroke penalty, on the other side of the hazard anywhere along a line which keeps the point of entry between him and the hole.

He does have one other—and better—option. He can place the ball on the green at the spot of his previous stroke (with, of course, a one-stroke penalty) and try the putt again. The option of replaying the previous stroke always exists for a ball in a water hazard (including lateral water), but is rarely used because it usually means a longer shot. In this case, though, it puts the ball not only closer to the hole, but on the green. It still may leave a treacherous putt, but it's probably easier than hitting across the water.

Now What If?

Bob yips a three-foot putt, which catches a downslope just past the hole and rolls into a greenside bunker. He declares the ball unplayable and replaces it where it lay three feet from the hole, with a one-stroke penalty. Is this permissible?

Yes. A player may declare his ball unplayable anywhere on the course except in a water hazard (Rule 28). The call is at the discretion of the player; "unplayable" doesn't mean it's physically impossible to play the shot. Since one of the options (all carrying a one-stroke penalty) for an unplayable ball is to replay the previous stroke, Bob is allowed to do so even though it puts the ball much closer to the hole than it was in the bunker.

Touch and Go

When can you touch the water or ground in a water hazard?

Ken hits his drive into a water hazard, but his ball is playable on the bank of the hazard. Before playing his ball, he sees another ball at the edge of the water and scoops it out with his club. He suddenly remembers that it is a penalty to touch the water or ground with a club in a hazard before playing a stroke from the hazard. Is he guilty of a violation?

There are exceptions under which a player is not penalized for touching the ground or water in a water hazard (Rule 13-4) before playing from the hazard. There is no penalty if it happens: 1) in placing clubs in a hazard; 2) as a result of falling, or to prevent falling; 3) in measuring or in retrieving or lifting a ball under any Rule; 4) in removing an obstruction; 5) in searching for the player's ball (Rule 12-1).

Obviously, numbers one and two have no bearing here. Number three doesn't apply either; Ken is retrieving a ball, but he's not doing so under a

Rule. Number five would help only if Ken thought the ball might be his; in this case, he didn't.

But what about number four? This is the one that gets Ken off the hook. According to Decision 24-1/2, an abandoned ball is an obstruction. Therefore, Ken is allowed to touch the water and ground with his club in the process of retrieving it.

Now What If?

Ken's ball lies on the bank of a water hazard. While waiting for another player to play, Ken casually leans on his club in the hazard. Is he penalized for touching the ground in the hazard?

Yes, Ken is penalized two strokes in stroke play or loss of hole in match play. None of the exceptions to Rule 13-4 apply.

Facing Danger

When is the face of a bunker part of the bunker?

Steve's approach shot ends up embedded in the face of a bunker. Is he entitled to relief?

The answer depends on whether the bunker face is grass-covered. If not, the ball is considered to be in the hazard (Rule 13). This means Steve does not get relief for an embedded ball, and if he declares the ball unplayable with a one-stroke penalty, he must drop it in the bunker unless he goes back to the point of his previous stroke.

If the face of the bunker is grass-covered, the ball is lying through the green and not in the hazard. Now Steve might be entitled to free relief under the right circumstances. Rule 25-2 allows a free drop if a ball is embedded in a closely mown area (fairway height or less) through the green. But even in longer grass, Steve gets relief if a Local Rule is in effect allowing a free drop for an embedded ball anywhere through the green. This Local Rule is common on U.S. courses and is in effect on the major Tours and in USGA events.

If Steve does get relief, it is possible the ball will roll away more than two club-lengths or into the hazard when he drops it, or not remain on the spot when he tries to place it after two tries at dropping. If the ball won't stay on the spot when placed, he places it at the nearest spot nearer to the hole and not in a hazard where it can be placed at rest (Rule 20).

Now What If?

In playing from a bunker, Steve touches a bare earth wall of the bunker with his club on his backswing. What is the ruling?

Steve is penalized two strokes in stroke play or loss of hole in match play for touching the ground in a hazard (Decision 13-4/34). The wall of the bunker is part of the hazard because it is not grass-covered. Steve would be permitted to touch an artificial wall (for example, railroad ties) with his club, but an earth wall is not artificial.

Double Trouble

What happens when a shot from a water hazard ends up out of bounds?

Greg hits his tee shot into a water hazard, but the ball is playable. He hits his next shot from where it lies in the hazard, and it goes out of bounds. What are his options?

Greg can proceed under the out-of-bounds Rule and drop another ball at the point inside the hazard where he just played from, taking a one-stroke penalty. He would be playing his fourth shot.

If he doesn't want to play his next shot from inside the hazard, two additional options allow him to proceed by taking an additional one-stroke penalty (Rule 26-2b). He can drop outside the hazard following the water hazard Rule, using the point where the *original* ball last crossed the margin of the hazard before it came to rest in the hazard as his reference point (dropping behind the hazard, keeping that point between him and the hole, or using the additional lateral water hazard options). Or, he can go back to the spot where he played his last stroke from outside the hazard (in this case, the tee) and play from there. If he uses one of these options to play from outside the hazard, his next stroke is his fifth, effectively taking his penalty for getting out of the hazard on top of the out-of-bounds penalty.

Now What If?

Greg hits his tee shot into a water hazard. He plays his next stroke from inside the hazard, and it goes out of bounds. He drops a ball inside the hazard, intending to take a one-stroke penalty and play his fourth stroke. The drop gives him a bad lie, and he decides he doesn't want to play from there. What are his options?

Greg takes an additional penalty of one stroke and either drops the ball outside the hazard, using the point where his original ball crossed the hazard line as his reference point, or goes back to the spot of his previous shot (the tee). He is playing his fifth stroke—the same as if he'd decided to use either of those options without taking a drop inside the hazard.

Choosing Sides

When you hit into a water hazard, you'd better know where to drop

Stuart's tee shot on a par three carries a water hazard fronting the green, marked by yellow stakes, but lands on the bank and rolls back into the water. He takes a penalty drop and plays his ball from the green side of the hazard. One of his fellow competitors, Terry, then says he thinks Stuart should have dropped the ball on the other side of the hazard. Stuart claims that since the ball landed past the hazard line, his drop was proper. Who is correct?

Terry is correct; Stuart should have dropped his ball on the tee side of the hazard, keeping the point where the ball last crossed the hazard line between him and the hole. The option of dropping within two club-lengths of where the ball last crossed the hazard line is available only for a lateral water hazard (marked by red stakes). Since this is a regular water hazard (yellow stakes), the fact that the ball landed past the hazard line before rolling back into the hazard is immaterial (Rule 26-1).

In stroke play, playing a stroke after dropping on the wrong side of the hazard is a serious breach of the Rule for playing from the wrong place (Rule 20-7), because the player gains a significant advantage. Stuart must rectify the error by playing from the right place and incurring a two-stroke penalty in addition to the one-stroke water hazard penalty. In match play, Stuart loses the hole for playing from the wrong place.

After hitting his ball into a water hazard in front of the green, Stuart incorrectly drops his ball on the green side of the hazard. Before Stuart plays a stroke, one of his fellow competitors, Terry, points out that Stuart has dropped in the wrong place. How does Stuart proceed?

Since he has not played from a wrong place, Stuart can pick up the ball without penalty (Rule 20-6) and drop in the right place, taking only the one-stroke water hazard penalty.

Second Stance

Prior to striking the ball, are you allowed to take a second stance in a greenside bunker?

Bill takes his stance in a greenside bunker, digging his feet into the sand. He then changes his mind about the type of shot to play and walks out of the bunker to change clubs. He returns to his ball, smooths out the original footprints, takes a new stance, and plays the shot. Is this allowed?

No. Bill is penalized two strokes in stroke play or loss of hole in match play for testing the condition of the hazard (Rule 13-4a). The Rules allow a player to place his feet firmly in taking a stance; in a bunker, this means it is all right to dig into the sand with your feet. But if his actions go beyond those necessary to take a stance in a bunker, and might help him determine the firmness of the sand, a player is subject to being penalized.

A player is allowed to take his stance in a bunker more than once. Bill would have been allowed to come back and take a new stance by placing his feet in the footprints he had already made, or by digging his feet in at a slightly different place without smoothing the first set of footprints.

Now What If?

Bill's ball is in a greenside bunker. He goes into the bunker without a club, digs into the sand with his feet, and simulates a stroke. He then gets a club, returns, digs in with his feet again at the same place, and plays his shot. Is this allowed?

If Bill went through this exercise in order to get a "feel" for the shot, and not to test the condition of the bunker, there is no penalty. When Bill first dug his feet into the sand, he met the definition of taking a stance, which is "placing his feet in position for and preparatory to making a stroke." However, a player is penalized if he digs in with his feet and simulates a stroke in a part of the bunker away from his ball.

Probing Question

Can a player be penalized for moving his ball in a hazard?

Carl hits his tee shot into a water hazard. While using a club to probe for his ball in the water, he accidentally kicks the ball, which is actually lying in long grass on the bank. Is there a penalty?

Carl is penalized one stroke in either stroke play or match play for moving his ball when it is in play (Rule 18-2a). He may replace the ball and play it, or, under an additional penalty of one stroke, take a drop under the water-hazard Rule.

There is no penalty for moving your ball *in water* in a water hazard when probing for it with a club, but Carl's ball isn't in the water and the movement of the ball isn't directly related to the probing. In any type of hazard, including bunkers, if a ball is covered by loose impediments or sand, a player is allowed to probe for it and is not penalized if the ball moves. However, in this case, the ball is covered only by grass.

With the above exceptions, a ball on the bank of a hazard is treated just like a ball on any other part of the course under Rule 18-2a—a player is penalized for causing his ball to move, except as permitted by a Rule (as in lifting it to proceed under the water-hazard Rule). So, be careful when

searching for your ball on the bank of a hazard. If you move it, you will be penalized one stroke, even if it is in such a bad lie that you wouldn't be able to play it.

Now What If?

Carl's fellow competitor, Tom, is probing for Carl's ball in the water inside a water hazard when he accidentally kicks the ball, which is actually lying on the bank of the hazard. Is there a penalty?

No. A fellow competitor is not penalized for moving a player's ball during a search (Rule 18-3a). There would also be no penalty if Tom is an opponent in match play. The ball is replaced.

Tidying Up

When should a player clean up his bunker mess?

Walter's ball is buried in a bunker. He searches for it by probing with a rake and eventually finds the ball. He restores the sand where he found the ball to its original condition and recreates the buried lie, then removes enough sand to leave part of the ball visible. He smooths the footprints he made while searching for the ball, and then plays his stroke. Is this procedure allowed?

A player is allowed to search for a ball in a bunker by probing for it with a rake, a club, or any other means, and he may remove enough sand to enable him to see part of the ball (Rule 12-1). There is no penalty if the ball is moved or if an excess of sand is removed; the ball should be replaced and re-covered with sand so that only part of the ball is visible.

Walter's procedure for finding the ball and restoring his lie is permissible. However, he incurs a penalty of two strokes in stroke play or loss of hole in match play for smoothing his footprints before playing his stroke. This is a violation of Rule 13-4, which does not allow the player to test the condition of a hazard or touch the ground in a hazard. Searching for a ball is an exception, but cleaning up after a search is not, so the player needs to wait until after the shot to clean up.

Now What If?

After searching for, and finding, Walter's ball in a bunker, Walter's caddie smooths the footprints made during the search before Walter plays his stroke. Is Walter penalized?

If the caddie smooths the footprints on his own initiative and the smoothing does not improve the lie of the ball or assist Walter in subsequent play of the hole, there is no penalty. If the caddie gives Walter information about the consistency of the sand based on the smoothing, Walter would be penalized two strokes in stroke play or loss of hole in match play.

Sand Blasting

It pays to keep your cool after a bad bunker shot

Playing from a greenside bunker, Tom doesn't get the ball out. He slams his club into the sand in disgust with his poor effort. Is he penalized for grounding his club in a hazard?

Yes. When a ball lies in a hazard, you can't touch the ground in the hazard with anything—club or otherwise (Rule 13-4). There are three exceptions, but none apply in this case. The club may touch an obstruction or anything growing (for example, grass) on the backswing, the player may place his clubs in a hazard, and the player may smooth sand or soil after making a stroke even if the ball still lies in the hazard. Slamming the club in a fit of anger does not count as smoothing the sand.

Incidentally, the exception for smoothing the sand only applies if it does not improve the lie of the ball or assist the golfer in playing the hole. If a subsequent shot rolls back into the smoothed area, the player is penalized.

Putting a different twist on Tom's situation, let's say his shot makes it to the grass bank of the bunker, he slams the club in disgust, and the ball then trickles back down the slope and into the bunker. This time he is not penalized for touching the sand because the prohibition applies only if the ball lies in the hazard. If, however, the club is still touching the sand when the ball rolls into the bunker, Tom is penalized. Decision 13-4/35.5 notes that any doubt about the timing should be resolved against the player.

Now What If?

Tom hits his bunker shot thin, sending it over the green and out of bounds on the other side. Before dropping a ball to play his next stroke from the bunker, he takes a couple of practice swings. Is he penalized for grounding his club in the hazard?

No. There is no penalty because the ball did not lie in the hazard when Tom touched the sand. Tom is free to take practice swings, hit the sand with his club in anger, or smooth his footprints so long as he does so before taking his drop.

CHAPTER FOUR

Out of Bounds/Lost Ball

Fenced In

Can a ball inside a boundary fence be out of bounds?

Lee's tee shot ends up resting against the inside of a chain-link fence, which marks the boundary of the course. Is the ball in bounds or out of bounds?

Most golfers would intuitively answer "in bounds." Actually, the answer depends on the diameter of the fence posts and whether the fence is bowed or straight. The definition of out of bounds (Rule 27) states that "the out-of-bounds line is determined by the inside points of the stakes or fence posts at ground level excluding angled supports." It also says that for a ball to be out of bounds, all of it must be out of bounds.

Thus, the out-of-bounds line, determined by the fence posts, might actually be a bit inside the line of the fence itself. But the ball is in bounds if any part of it is inside the out-of-bounds line. One general statement can safely be made: If the posts of a boundary fence are on the golf course side of the fence, the diameter of the posts is greater than the diameter of the golf ball, and the fence is straight, then a ball lying against the inside of the fence is out of bounds (Decision 27/20).

If the fence is bowed inward, it's more likely the ball will be inside the fence posts, and thus in bounds. But if it is bowed outward, there's a very good chance the ball is out of bounds.

Now What If?

Lee's tee shot ends up resting against the inside of a chain-link fence, which marks the boundary of the course. The ball is ruled in bounds. On his next stroke, does he get relief from the fence, which interferes with his swing?

No. The definition of an "obstruction," from which a player gets free relief (Rule 24), says objects defining out of bounds are not obstructions. If Lee needs to move the ball away from the fence to play it, he must declare the ball unplayable and take a one-stroke penalty.

Too Late?

Reaching the point of no return on a lost ball

Bill hooks his approach shot into dense woods to the left of the green. After briefly looking for the ball, he returns to the spot of his previous stroke and drops another. Before he plays the dropped ball, and less than five minutes after the search began, one of his fellow competitors finds Bill's original ball. Is Bill allowed to pick up the dropped ball and play the original?

No, because his original ball is considered lost as soon as Bill drops another ball. A ball is defined as "lost" (Rule 27) if: 1) it is not found within five minutes of the beginning of the search; 2) the player has put another ball in play under the Rules; 3) the player has played a stroke with a provisional ball from where the original ball is likely to be.

A ball dropped under an applicable Rule becomes the ball in play as soon as it is dropped (Rule 20-4). Therefore, Bill has "put another ball in play" under the lost-ball Rule even before playing a stroke with the dropped ball.

It should be noted that the ball isn't considered lost when Bill stops searching for it. Even if he declares it lost, it's not officially lost until he puts another ball in play (or the five minutes elapses). If it had been found before he dropped the second ball, he could have played the original. Of course, he could have saved himself the problem by hitting a provisional ball in the first place.

Now What If?

Bill hits his drive into the woods, looks for it briefly, then returns to the teeing ground and tees up another ball. Before he plays the second ball, and less than five minutes after the search began, the original ball is found. Is Bill allowed to abandon the teed ball and play the original?

Yes. The original ball is not lost until the player puts another ball in play. The Rules define a ball to be "in play" as soon as the player makes a stroke from the teeing ground. Simply teeing up a ball does not put it in play.

Provisional Problems

What do you do if a provisional ball can't be distinguished from the original?

Ted hits his first drive into the trees, where it might be lost. He plays a provisional ball, but forgets to play one with different markings. He hits the provisional ball in the same general area as the original. Both balls are found in bounds, but they are not distinguishable from each other. What is the ruling?

It could be argued that both balls are lost, but it would be inequitable for the player to have to return to the tee, playing five. Therefore, the ruling is that Ted selects one ball, treats it as his provisional, and abandons the other (Decision 27/11).

The player isn't getting a break by being able to choose which ball to play. If the ball he chooses really is the original, he's losing two strokes. And if the ball really is the provisional, chances are he would have been better off playing the original without penalty even if it is in a worse lie.

If one or both balls are found in a water hazard, it complicates the situation because a provisional ball must be abandoned if the original is found in a water hazard. If both balls are found in a water hazard or if one is found in a water hazard and the other is found outside the hazard and in bounds, the player must return to the tee and play another ball (playing three).

If one is found in a water hazard and the other is not found, the ball in the hazard is presumed to be the provisional.

Now What If?

Ted hits his original ball and a provisional in the same general area. The balls cannot be distinguished from one another. One ball is found in bounds and the other ball is either lost or found out of bounds. What is the ruling?

Ted proceeds with the ball in bounds, which must be presumed to be the provisional ball.

Delayed Search

Can a player tell his caddie to wait before looking for his ball?

Jason hits a long drive into heavy rough to the right of the fairway and Todd hits a shorter drive into the right rough. Jason's caddie starts walking toward the area where his ball is likely to be. Everyone else, including Jason, begins to search for Todd's ball. Jason directs his caddie to join the search for Todd's ball and not look for his ball until everyone can assist. Is this allowed?

Yes. The five-minute period allowed for finding a ball starts as soon as anyone on the player's side or his or their caddies begins to search for it (Rule 27). Thus, if Jason's caddie begins his search for Jason's ball while everyone else is searching for Todd's ball, that time counts against Jason. If Jason is concerned that his ball might be difficult to find, he is within his rights to tell his caddie to wait until everyone can help look for his ball.

The situation is similar if a caddie is acting as a forecaddie and begins to search for his player's ball while the players are walking from the tee. If

the ball is not found within five minutes of the time the *caddie* begins to search for it, the ball is lost. However, if the forecaddie is a fellow competitor's caddie, or if spectators at a tournament begin to look for a ball, the five-minute clock doesn't start until the player or his caddie (or anyone on the player's side or their caddies in a team match) joins the search.

Now What If?

Jason hits his drive into heavy rough to the right of the fairway and also hits his provisional ball into the right rough. Is he allowed five minutes to search for his original ball and five minutes to search for the provisional, or just a total of five minutes?

If the two balls are so close together that, in effect, both balls would be searched for simultaneously, a total of five minutes is allowed. Otherwise, Jason would be allowed to search five minutes for each ball.

Thrown for a Loss

What happens when you find your ball, but don't know it?

Steve and Paul are searching for their balls in the same area of the rough. After two minutes, Steve finds a ball, which he believes is Paul's, and resumes his search. After the five-minute search period elapses, it is discovered that the ball Steve found was in fact his own, not Paul's. What is the ruling?

Steve's ball is considered to be "lost," and he must take a stroke-and-distance penalty and return to the spot of his previous stroke. (If he already has played a provisional ball, it becomes his ball in play.)

According to Rule 27, a ball is lost if it is not found or identified as his by the player within five minutes after the player's side or his or their caddies have begun to search for it. Once a ball has been found, the player has an opportunity to identify it as his. In this case, Steve had every chance to identify the ball as his within the five-minute period, and failed to do so. The only situation in which a player could escape a lost-ball penalty by identifying his ball after the five-minute period would be if somebody else

found the ball within five minutes, but the player didn't have a chance to identify it until after the five minutes had elapsed.

Now What If?

Steve and Paul are searching for their balls in the same area of the rough. After two minutes, Steve finds a ball, which he believes to be Paul's. The five-minute search period elapses without any more balls being found. Paul then plays the ball from the rough, but as he prepares for his next stroke, he realizes the ball he played was Steve's. What is the ruling?

In match play, Paul loses the hole for playing a wrong ball (Rule 15-2). In stroke play, Paul is penalized two strokes for playing the wrong ball (Rule 15-3) and must correct his mistake; both Paul and Steve must take stroke-and-distance penalties for lost balls.

Compounding the Error

Breaking multiple Rules can lead to a big penalty

Bob hits his tee shot into the woods. Fearing the ball is lost, he hits a provisional. Bob finds a ball he believes to be his original, plays it, and picks up his provisional ball. When he prepares for his next stroke, he discovers that the ball he played was not his original, but a wrong ball. He resumes his search for the original ball, but can't find it. What is the ruling?

In stroke play, Bob is required to replace his provisional ball and play out with it. Since he has lost a ball and broken two other Rules, he is playing his seventh stroke after replacing the ball (Decision 27-2b/9). In match play, he simply loses the hole for playing a wrong ball.

The wrong-ball penalty in stroke play is two strokes (Rule 15-3). Since he can't find the original ball, he is assessed the stroke-and-distance penalty under Rule 27-1, making the provisional the ball in play. That ball is now in his pocket; by lifting a ball that was to become the ball in play, he has incurred a one-stroke penalty under Rule 18-2a, the same as if he had lifted a ball that actually was in play.

It could be worse. If he goes back to the tee and plays from there instead of replacing the provisional ball, he is playing his eighth stroke. In this case, he incurs the general penalty of two strokes under Rule 18 instead of one stroke under Rule 18-2a.

Now What If?

In stroke play, Bob plays a wrong ball, discovers his error, and returns to the area he played the wrong ball from. He finds another ball, plays it, and discovers he has played another wrong ball. Is he penalized two strokes or four strokes?

The penalty is two strokes for breach of the wrong-ball Rule. Decision 15-3/2 rules that a penalty of four strokes for playing two wrong balls in succession before a stroke with the correct ball would not be justified. (In match play, he loses the hole by playing the first wrong ball.)

CHAPTER FIVE

On the Green

Is This a Test?

A roll of a ball might or might not constitute testing

Bill's putt from 20 feet stops within inches of the hole. His match-play opponent, Chris, concedes the putt and knocks the ball back to Bill with a one-handed swing of the putter. Bill then claims he has won the hole because Chris violated Rule 16-1/d, which says a player "shall not test the surface of the putting green by rolling a ball or roughening or scraping the surface."Is Bill correct?

No. There is no violation, because the casual act of returning a ball to a player on a conceded putt, either by picking it up and rolling it or knocking it back with a club, is not considered to be testing the surface (Decision 16-1d/1).

However, if a player knocks a conceded putt back on the line of his own upcoming putt, a breach has occurred if the intent was to test the surface

(Decision 16-1d/2). Even if a player does not admit his intent, the manner and apparent purpose of the action determine whether a penalty should be applied in a particular case.

The Rule for testing the putting surface allows some leniency in interpretation. Other actions that might be questioned but do not draw a penalty are cleaning a ball by rubbing it on the green and checking the wetness of the putting surface by placing your hand on the green (as long as it is not done on the line of the putt and you do not roughen or scrape the surface with your hand).

Now What If?

Chris marks his ball on the green. When it is his turn to putt, he returns the ball back to its spot by rolling it with his putter. Is he penalized for testing the putting surface?

No, provided the rolling was not done for the purpose of testing the surface. Decision 16-1d/3 goes on to say that this method of returning the ball is not recommended, though it is not a breach of the Rules.

Let It Be

When is a player not allowed to immediately repair his pitch-mark?

Lee and Paul both hit the green with their approach shots. Paul's ball is closer to the hole. His pitch-mark is near Lee's line. Paul is getting ready to repair his pitch-mark when Lee stops him, saying he wants the pitch-mark left alone because it is so situated that it might deflect Lee's ball into the hole. Paul says he thinks he should be allowed to repair the pitch-mark immediately. Is Paul allowed to do so?

No. If Paul were to repair the pitch-mark after being asked not to, he would violate Rule 1-2, which says that a player shall not take any action to influence the position or movement of a ball except in accordance with the Rules. The penalty is two strokes in stroke play or loss of hole in match play. Paul must wait until Lee putts before repairing the pitch-mark.

If, however, Lee doesn't say anything beforehand, Paul isn't penalized for repairing the pitch-mark. It is only Lee's objection that creates the motive for a violation of Rule 1-2. Also, if it were Paul's turn to play and the pitch-mark affected his play, he would be allowed to repair the pitch-mark. A similar situation can arise in the case of loose impediments. If a player feels that loose impediments are in a position where they could help him, such as stones or leaves behind the hole on a downhill putt, and he requests that an opponent or fellow competitor not remove them, it is a breach of Rule 1-2 to remove them.

Now What If?

Paul marks his ball on the green and the ball marker is in a position where it might help Lee line up his putt. Paul prepares to move his ball marker one clubhead-length to the side, but Lee says he wants the ball marker left where it is. Is Paul allowed to move the ball marker?

Yes. In view of the purposes of Rule 8-2b ("no mark shall be placed anywhere to indicate a line for putting") and Rule 22a ("any player may lift his ball if he considers that the ball might assist any other player"), Lee cannot insist the ball marker be left as it is.

Obstacle Course

What happens when the ball strikes the hole-liner?

Scott is attending the flagstick for Bill, whose ball lies on the green. Scott tries to remove the flagstick as Bill's putt approaches the hole, but the flagstick is stuck in the bottom of the hole. When Scott pulls on the flagstick, he yanks the hole-liner out of the hole, and Bill's ball strikes the hole-liner. Is there a penalty?

No. While a penalty is involved if a ball played from the green strikes the flagstick, whether attended or unattended, the hole-liner is not part of the flagstick. The hole-liner is an outside agency (Decision 17/8). If the hole-liner was moving when the ball struck it, the stroke is canceled and replayed (Rule 19-1b). However, if the hole-liner was not moving, or if the ball was not played from the green, the stroke counts and the ball must be played as it lies (Rule 19-1).

If the hole-liner had not been pulled above the level of the hole and the ball had struck the flagstick instead, Bill would have been penalized two strokes in stroke play or loss of hole in match play, and the ball would have been played as it lies (Rule 17-3). When the flagstick is being attended with the authority of the player, the penalty for striking it falls on the player making the stroke, not on the attendant, even though it is the attendant's mistake.

Now What If?

On Bill's putt to a hole where the flagstick has been removed, the ball strikes the rim of the hole-liner, which had not been sunk deep enough, and bounces out of the hole. Is the ball considered holed?

No. A ball is not considered holed until it is at rest within the circumference of the hole (Rule 16). If the hole-liner is sunk at least one inch below the surface of the green, as the Rules suggest, this should not happen.

On the Edge

Can a player try to make a ball hanging on the lip drop in?

Jeff's putt comes to rest overhanging the edge of the hole. Jeff walks up to the hole and casts his shadow on the ball, believing that this could cause the ball to fall into the hole. Is he penalized for exerting influence on the ball?

There is no penalty, even if the ball falls into the hole. While some believe that casting a shadow on a ball hanging on the lip can cause the grass to

wilt and the ball to drop, the USGA doesn't buy it. Rule 1-2 states that no player or caddie shall take any action to influence the position or movement of a ball except in accordance with the Rules, but casting a shadow on the ball is allowed by Decision 16-2/3.

On the other hand, a player is penalized under Rule 1-2 if he jumps close to the hole and causes a ball overhanging the lip to drop. If the ball was moving when the player jumped—or if it was impossible to determine if the ball was moving—he loses the hole in match play or is penalized two strokes in stroke play (the ball is considered holed). If the ball was at rest when the player jumped, it is assumed the player caused the ball to move, and he is penalized one stroke in either match play or stroke play under Rule 18-2a and is required to replace the ball.

Now What If?

In a match between Jeff and Doug, Jeff's putt ends up overhanging the lip of the hole. Within five seconds, Doug concedes Jeff's next stroke and knocks the ball away. Is this allowed?

No. Jeff is allowed a reasonable time to reach the hold and an additional 10 seconds to determine whether the ball is at rest (Rule 16-2). Since Doug infringed on that right, he loses the hole (or halves the hole if he has already holed out and Jeff's putt was for a half).

Spiked Up

Can you fix spike marks made by a player walking in your line?

Jason's ball is marked with a coin on the green. His fellow competitor, Glen, unwittingly steps in the line of Jason's putt, leaving spike marks. What is the ruling?

Since the line of putt has been damaged, it may be restored to its previous condition by tapping down the spike marks. This is allowed under the principle that a player is entitled to the lie and line of putt he had when the ball came to rest. The line of putt may be restored by anyone. If the damage is so severe that the line cannot be restored, the player can ask the committee in charge of the competition for relief, and the committee can declare the area to be ground under repair.

If Glen had purposely stepped on Jason's line, he would have been penalized under Rule 1-2 for taking an action to influence the movement of a ball. This would be the case whether he did so with the intention of improving the line (such as by pressing down a raised tuft of grass) or of damaging it by making spike marks. The penalty is loss of hole in match play or two strokes in stroke play. If the committee rules that it was a serious breach, it can impose a penalty of disqualification.

Now What If?

Jason unwittingly steps in the line of his own putt. Does he incur a penalty under Rule 16-1a for touching his line of putt?

No, if his stepping in the line didn't improve the line. However, if he damaged the line by doing so, he is not entitled to restore the line to its previous condition. If his accidental stepping improved the line, or if he intentionally stepped in the line, Jason is penalized two strokes in stroke play or loss of hole in match play. A player is prohibited from touching the line of putt, with several exceptions (such as to move sand or loose impediments) that don't apply here.

Poor Attendance

What's the ruling when a flagstick attendant screws up?

Jeff is playing in the club championship. Facing a long putt, he calls a spectator to attend the flagstick. The spectator is distracted during the putt, and the ball hits his foot. What is the ruling?

In stroke play, Jeff is penalized two strokes and the ball is played as it lies (Rule 17-3). In match play, Jeff loses the hole. The penalty also applies if the ball strikes the flagstick when attended (or when unattended when the ball is played from the green).

The ruling is the same no matter who is attending the flagstick, as long as the attendance is with the player's authority or prior knowledge. Anyone may attend the flagstick, including a partner, caddie, opponent, fellow competitor, spectator, even a greenkeeper. The one exception: A referee or observer should not attend the flagstick.

A fellow competitor, opponent, or their caddie can attend the flagstick only with the player's authority. If any of them does so without authority and the ball strikes the attendant or the flagstick, the fellow competitor or

opponent suffers a two-stroke or loss-of-hole penalty. In stroke play, the stroke is canceled and replayed if the ball was played from the putting green. However, if someone attends the flagstick prior to the stroke with the player's knowledge and no objection is made, the player is deemed to have authorized it.

Now What If?

Jeff calls on a spectator to attend the flagstick during the club championship. Jeff's putt stops a couple of inches from the hole; the spectator then kicks the ball away. What is the ruling?

Since the ball came to rest, there is no penalty for the ball striking the flagstick attendant. The spectator is an outside agency, so Jeff replaces the ball without penalty and holes out (in match play, of course, his opponent could concede the putt).

On a Roll

Todd's ball finishes on the green, 15 feet away from the hole. He lifts and cleans it, then replaces it. As he studies his putt, the ball, which is lying on a slope, rolls about five feet closer to the hole. Does he replace the ball to its original position or play it from where it stopped rolling?

If the ball remained at rest for a few seconds, Todd plays it from where it ended up after rolling closer to the hole. Once it is at rest, the ball is in play. Neither gravity nor wind—the forces that might have moved the ball in this situation—are considered outside agencies, so the ball is not replaced (Rule 18). If Todd is lucky enough to have the ball roll into the hole, he is considered to have holed out with his previous stroke. However, if the ball didn't start moving until after Todd addressed it, he is considered to have caused it to move, is penalized one stroke, and must replace the ball (Rule 18-2b).

In the original situation, Todd must replace the ball if it was not at rest before it started rolling down the slope. If he is unable to put the ball back

on the green so that it stays at rest, he places it at the nearest spot not nearer the hole where it can be placed at rest (Rule 20-3d).

Now What If?

After his second shot, an approach to a par four, Todd's ball is overhanging the lip of the hole. There is mud on the ball, so Todd marks his ball, cleans it, and replaces it. The ball remains on the lip of the hole for a few seconds, then falls into the hole. What is the ruling?

Todd makes a three on the hole. Rule 16-2 specifically covers the situation of a ball overhanging the hole. If a ball falls into the hole after being deemed to be at rest overhanging the lip, the player is considered to have holed out with his previous stroke, but he also must add a penalty stroke. In this case, the ball must be considered to have been at rest when it was replaced; otherwise it would have to be replaced again (Rule 20-3d).

CHAPTER SIX

Ball Moved or Deflected

Sorry About That

Is there a penalty when a ball strikes another player?

Tom hits his tee shot off the toe of his club. The ball flies off at a right angle to its intended line and hits Matt, Tom's match-play opponent, on the shin. Is there any penalty? Where does Tom play his next stroke from?

While the situation is embarrassing for Tom and painful for Matt, there is no penalty on either player if a ball is accidentally deflected or stopped by an opponent, his caddie, or his equipment (Rule 19-3). However, Matt is, in a sense, penalized for getting in the way of the ball because Tom has the option of canceling the stroke and playing his tee shot again. If the ball had struck another member of the foursome who was not in the match, Tom would have had to play the ball from where it lies.

If, on the other hand, the ball strikes Tom's partner (or his partner's caddie or equipment) in a team match, Tom suffers a loss-of-hole penalty, which means he would be disqualified from the hole. If the ball strikes Tom's equipment, such as his golf bag, his caddie, or himself, he is disqualified from the hole in a team match or loses the hole in a singles match. Another instance in which a player is penalized is when his ball strikes the person tending the flagstick, in which case it doesn't matter whether the person is an opponent, partner, or outside agency (Rule 17-3b). The only time an opponent is penalized for deflecting the ball is if he does so intentionally (Rule 1-2).

Nutty Situation

What to do when a squirrel runs away with a ball from an undetermined spot

Gene hits his tee shot on a par-three hole to the right of the green into an area that can't be seen from the tee. In this area are fairway, a bunker, light rough, and deep rough. As Gene reaches this area, he sees a squirrel has picked up a ball and is running away with it. The squirrel drops the ball, and Gene identifies it as his. How should Gene proceed?

Gene's ball has been moved by an outside agency, so according to Rule 18-1 he incurs no penalty and replaces the ball where it lay after his tee shot. This situation is not quite so simple, however, because he never saw where the ball came to rest.

Ball Moved or Deflected   **59**

According to Rule 20-3, if it is impossible to determine the exact spot where the ball is to be replaced, the ball shall be dropped as near as possible to where it lay. This is still not enough to solve Gene's dilemma. He's not even sure whether his ball was in the fairway, the bunker, or the rough.

Decision 18-1/5 gives the answer by invoking equity (Rule 1-4). When it is impossible to know where the ball should be replaced, the player should drop the ball in an area which is neither the most, nor the least, favorable of the various areas where it was equally possible that the ball originally lay. In this case, that means a pitch from the light rough.

Now What If?

Gene's tee shot on a par three hole ends up in an area that can't be seen from the tee. The ball might have come to rest in the fairway, a bunker, light rough, or deep rough. As he approaches the area, Gene sees a squirrel running away with a ball but is unable to recover the ball to identify it as his. How should he proceed?

Gene must consider the ball lost and take a stroke-and-distance penalty (Rule 27). If the area were all fairway, he would be justified in saying there was reasonable evidence his ball was moved by an outside agency. But since it's possible his ball was lost in the deep rough, seeing a squirrel run away with a ball is not sufficient evidence.

Deliberate Deflection

What happens when a spectator swats a ball away?

Steve is playing in a tournament. On the 16th hole, he pulls his approach shot well left of the green toward a bank that leads down to a water hazard. A spectator deliberately deflects the ball, keeping it near the green where Steve has an easy pitch shot. Should the ball be played as it lies?

No. Normally when an outside agency, such as a spectator, deflects or stops a ball in motion, the ball is played as it lies. But a note under Rule 19-1 makes an exception if an outside agency purposely deflects or stops a ball. In such a case, it's up to the referee or committee to make an equitable ruling as to where the ball would have ended up; the player drops the ball at that spot. This ruling goes into effect only if it's clear the deflection or stop was purposeful. If a spectator deflects a ball when he puts his hands up

to protect himself from being hit, that's not purposeful. If he takes two steps toward the ball and leaps to swat at it with his hand, that's purposeful.

Decision 19-1/4.1 instructs the committee to give the player the benefit of doubt in determining where to drop the ball. If the ball might have been accidentally stopped or deflected by another spectator standing behind the offending spectator, the ball is dropped at the point of the deflection. If the ball would clearly have come to rest somewhere else, the committee must make a judgment. For example, if the ball would have come to rest either in a hazard or in rough just short of the hazard, the player should drop the ball in the rough.

Now What If?

Steve plays a stroke from the green and, while the ball is still moving, a spectator runs onto the putting surface and deliberately deflects or stops the ball. What is the ruling?

The stroke is canceled, the ball replaced, and the stroke replayed, without penalty.

Wrong Place, Wrong Time

What happens when a caddie can't get out of the way of a ball?

Brian's caddie is serving as a forecaddie on the ninth hole. Brian's drive sails way to the right and the ball hits his caddie, who is standing in bounds. The ball ends up out of bounds. What is the ruling?

In stroke play, Brian must retee the ball and is playing his fifth stroke because he is penalized two strokes for having his ball deflected by his caddie (Rule 19-2) in addition to stroke-and-distance for the ball finishing out of bounds. In match play, more mercifully, he simply loses the hole under Rule 19-2.

The player is penalized if his ball deflects off his caddie whether the caddie is in bounds or out of bounds. And, in either case, the result of the shot stands. If the ball accidentally deflects off the caddie and ends up in bounds, the player is penalized two strokes in stroke play and plays the ball as it lies, even if the caddie was out of bounds. The same rulings hold true if the ball is deflected by a player's equipment, which might occur when the configuration of a course allows players to leave their bags or carts in the landing area of their drives (a cart shared by two players is deemed to be the equipment of the player whose ball is involved unless the cart is in motion with another player driving).

If the ball is deflected by an outside agency, such as the caddie of a fellow competitor in stroke play, there is no penalty and the result of the shot stands.

Now What If?

In match play, Brian's drive is deflected by his opponent's caddie, who is acting as a forecaddie, and the ball finishes out of bounds. What is the ruling?

There is no penalty on the opponent. However, Brian has the option of canceling the stroke and replaying his first stroke from the tee (Rule 19-3), which he certainly would do if the ball ends up out of bounds.

Bump on the Green

Is it a good break when a ball at rest is knocked into the hole?

Ira's ball is sitting on the green a few feet from the hole. Mike hits a pitch shot from some distance off the green; his ball strikes Ira's ball and knocks it into the hole. Mike's ball ends up a few feet from the hole. Is Ira's ball considered to be holed?

No. When a ball at rest is moved by a ball in motion after a stroke, the moved ball is replaced while the deflected ball is played as it lies (Rules 18-5 and 19-5). This applies even if the moved ball ends up in the hole. Therefore, Ira must replace his ball as near as possible to the spot where it lay while Mike plays from where his ball ended up.

In stroke play, if Ira fails to replace his ball, he must correct his mistake before teeing off on the next hole or be disqualified for failure to hole out.

In match play, if Ira doesn't replace his ball because both players are ignorant of the Rules, the hole stands once either player tees off on the next hole.

If it had been Mike's ball that ended up in the hole after the deflection, his ball would be considered to have been holed. That's why Rule 22 gives a player the right to lift his ball if he thinks the ball might assist another player. In this case, however, the players were too far from the green for Ira to mark his ball.

Now What If?

Ira and Mike hit their shots from off the green at nearly the same time. The balls strike each other while both are still moving, and Ira's ball ends up in the hole. Is his ball considered to be holed?

Yes. When a player's ball in motion after a stroke is deflected by another ball in motion, the ball is played as it lies—and in this case is considered holed.

Off the Mark

What happens if a ball is marked, but not replaced?

In stroke play, John plays his ball from a greenside bunker onto the green, where it ends up in Bill's putting line. Bill marks John's ball and places it nearby on the green. John, unaware that his ball was marked and moved, putts the ball from where it lies and holes out. What is the ruling?

Since John did not know that Bill lifted his ball, John is not penalized (Decision 15-3/3). If John becomes aware of the mistake before playing from the next tee, he is required to replace his ball on the correct spot, without penalty, and complete the hole. If he learns of the mistake after playing from the next tee, his score stands and there is no penalty.

If John were aware that Bill had lifted his ball, he would have been penalized two strokes and required to replace his ball on the correct spot and play out the hole. When the ball is lifted, it is no longer the ball in play until it is returned to the proper place, and is technically a wrong ball.

In match play, Bill would be penalized one stroke for marking John's

ball without authorization (Rule 18-3b) and would lose the hole if he allowed John to play without replacing the ball. If John authorizes Bill to mark the ball, John loses the hole if he then plays the ball from where it lies after Bill set it aside.

Now What If?

John plays a blind tee shot into the rough. After his ball comes to rest, some children playing near the course move his ball into the fairway. John is not aware the ball has been moved, so he does not replace it. He finishes the hole, tees off at the next hole, and then learns that his ball was moved at the previous hole. What is the ruling?

Since John did not know that his ball was moved, it would be inequitable to impose a penalty for failure to replace a ball moved by an outside agency (Decision 18-1/3). His score with the moved ball stands.

CHAPTER SEVEN

Dropping/Placing

Sticky Situation

What do you do when a ball marker doesn't stay put?

Brad marks his ball on the green with a coin, lifts the ball, and, using the sole of his putter, presses down the coin so it is less likely to interfere with (or assist) the play of another player. As Brad walks away, he notices that the coin has stuck to his putter. Is he penalized for moving the ball marker?

There is no penalty, and Brad replaces the marker as close as possible to the original spot (or on the precise spot if it can be identified). Rule 20-1 states, "If a ball or a ball marker is accidentally moved in the process of lifting the ball under a Rule or marking its position, the ball or ball marker shall be replaced. There is no penalty provided the movement ... is directly attributable to the specific act of marking the position of or lifting the ball." Pressing down the marker with the putter is considered part of the process of marking the ball according to Decision 20-1/6.

In the more common applications, this Rule acts as a safeguard against clumsiness. If the player accidentally knocks the ball forward with his hand while placing the coin down, or moves the marker as he sweeps up the ball, he is not penalized.

Now What If?

Brad marks his ball on the green with a coin and lifts the ball. When it's his turn to play, he can't find his ball marker. Eventually, he finds it stuck to the sole of his shoe and concludes that he stepped on the coin while helping his partner line up a putt. Is he penalized for moving the ball marker?

Brad is penalized one stroke in either match play or stroke play (Decision 20-1/5.5). The ball marker wasn't moved in the process of lifting or marking the ball, so he is not exempt from penalty under that provision.

Double Drop

What happens when you need relief from two conditions?

Greg's tee shot comes to rest on a paved cart path. He decides to take a drop and determines that his nearest point of relief from the cart path is in casual water next to the path. How should he proceed?

Greg must first drop the ball within one club-length of his nearest point of relief, even though that point is in casual water. If, after the drop, casual water interferes with his stance or the area of his intended swing, he has the option of playing the ball as it lies or taking a second drop away from casual water. (The reverse is also true. If a player hits his ball into casual water and the nearest point of relief is on a cart path, he must drop on the cart path.)

The Rules generally do not allow for taking relief from two conditions in one step; it must be done separately. This is true even if the ball lies in two conditions at once, such as casual water within ground under repair. If the player wants to take relief in this case, he chooses to take his first drop from either condition. After the drop, he has the option of playing the ball as it lies (unless the first condition interferes) or taking another drop away from the second condition.

Now What If?

Greg's tee shot comes to rest on a paved cart path. He takes relief from the path and drops in casual water next to the path. His nearest point of relief from casual water is back on the path. How should he proceed?

In addition to the options of dropping back on the path or playing the ball as it lies, Decision 1-4/8 allows the player, in equity, to obtain relief at the point nearest to the ball's original position on the cart path which is no closer to the hole, avoids interference with both the cart path and the casual water, and is not in a hazard or on a putting green.

Forward Roll

Knowing whether to re-drop can be tricky

John's ball is under a tree, and he declares it unplayable. He takes his drop about 10 yards behind where the ball lay, keeping that point between the hole and the drop point. When he drops the ball, it rolls about a yard closer to the hole than where it struck the ground. Is he required to re-drop?

No. The drop is fine (assuming the ball hasn't rolled into or out of a hazard, out of bounds, or onto a putting green) and the ball is now in play (Rule 20-2). In fact, John is penalized if he re-drops—or even picks up—the ball.

This is a point of confusion for many players. It's commonly thought a re-drop is required if the ball rolls nearer to the hole after striking the ground. Actually, a re-drop is required if the ball ends up nearer to the hole than its original position (in this case, where the ball lay when it was declared unplayable) or more than two club-lengths from where it struck the ground. John's ball meets neither condition after his drop.

The penalty is one stroke in either stroke play or match play if John lifts his ball, realizes he's made a mistake, and replaces it (Rule 18-2). If he re-drops the ball and plays from the wrong place, the total penalty is two strokes in stroke play or loss of hole in match play (Rule 20-7).

Now What If?

John's ball is under a tree, and he declares it unplayable. He takes his drop behind a bunker; the ball rolls towards the hole and ends up in the bunker. Is he required to re-drop?

Yes—because the ball ended up in a bunker. A re-drop is required if the ball rolls into a hazard, and a bunker is considered a hazard.

On the Spot

When replacing a ball, do you drop it or place it?

Dave hits his approach shot into a greenside bunker. One of his fellow competitors then hits his shot into the same bunker; his ball strikes Dave's ball, which rolls down a slope after the contact. Dave is required to replace the ball at its original spot. Does he drop the ball or place it?

This actually happened to Dave Stockton in the final round of the 1994 Senior Players Championship. It was ruled he could place the ball, but only because the balls left trails in the sand enabling the original spot to be determined exactly.

When a ball at rest is moved by another ball that has been struck, the moved ball is replaced and the other ball is played from where it came to rest (Rules 18-5 and 19-5). But, in any situation where a ball is replaced through the green or in a hazard, the player is allowed to place the ball only if the *precise* spot is determinable. If only an approximate spot is known, the ball must be dropped (Rule 20-3c) unless it is on the green, in which case it is placed.

Usually when a ball is hit and moved by a moving ball, only an approximate spot is known because the witnesses are some distance away. Such would have been the case for Stockton, except for the "ball tracks" in the sand that enabled him to avoid the less-than-perfect lie he would have gotten if a drop had been necessary.

Now What If?

Dave's ball, which lies on the fringe, moves when it is hit by a ball struck by a fellow competitor. He is required to drop the ball because the original spot is not determinable, but he places it instead. Before hitting his next shot, he realizes his mistake and drops the ball. Is he penalized?

No. A player is allowed to correct his error for dropping or placing the ball improperly or in a wrong place (Rule 20-6). If he had played the ball, Dave would have been penalized two strokes in stroke play or loss of hole in match play.

Branching Out

When dropping, a tree branch is like any other part of the course

Rob hits his ball into the trees and declares the ball unplayable. When he drops within two club-lengths of the ball's original position, the ball strikes a tree branch and hits the ground outside the prescribed dropping area. Is a re-drop required?

Not necessarily. The Rules require the ball to strike the course, not the ground, within the dropping area, and the branch is part of the course (Rule 20-2). Therefore, the ball is in play and must not be re-dropped, unless it rolls into a position where a re-drop is required — such as more than two club-lengths from where it struck the course or nearer to the hole than its original position. In measuring the two club-lengths, the point on the ground immediately below where the ball struck the branch is used. The player is not allowed to have a caddie (or anyone else) hold back a branch to prevent it from deflecting a dropped ball.

You might wonder why a player would drop his ball under a tree. In the case of an unplayable lie, where the original position of the ball offers no hope, it might at least give the player a swing. In other situations, such as dropping away from a cart path or casual water, free relief is given at a specific point. Since natural obstacles are not considered in this determination, the point of relief might be under a tree.

Now What If?

Rob takes a drop after declaring his ball unplayable. When dropped, the ball lodges in a bush within the prescribed dropping area, without striking the ground. Does Rob get a re-drop?

No. The ball is in play, and Rob must either play it from there or declare his ball unplayable again. The ball struck a part of the course in the required area, and did not roll into a position requiring it to be re-dropped. The ruling is the same for a drop under any Rule.

CHAPTER EIGHT

Abnormal Ground Conditions

Casual Quandary

What do you do when a bunker is filled with casual water?

Tom hits his ball into a bunker that is completely covered by casual water. His ball lies in water too deep to play a shot. He takes relief by dropping within the bunker at a point where the water is very shallow. His opponent, Frank, says that is not allowed because a player must take complete relief. Who is correct?

Tom's procedure is allowed because the ball is in a bunker. Through the green, a player taking relief from casual water (or ground under repair) must drop at a point that avoids interference by the condition, both in his stance and the area of his swing. This means he can't move to a spot where there is less casual water. In a hazard, however, he may drop at a point that provides "maximum available relief" (Rule 25-1b).

The reason is that when the ball is in a hazard, free relief is allowed only if the drop is within the hazard. A drop outside the hazard (keeping the point where the ball lay between the hole and the drop point) incurs a one-stroke penalty. Rather than forcing a player to take a penalty stroke in a situation where a bunker is filled with casual water, the Rules provide the option of taking relief where there is the least interference. If an area in the bunker provides complete relief no closer to the hole, the player must drop there, because that constitutes "maximum available relief."

Now What If?

Tom hits his ball into a bunker completely covered by casual water. He takes a drop in the bunker at a point that affords maximum available relief. When dropped, the ball rolls from a spot with about a quarter inch of casual water to a spot where the water is about a half-inch deep. What is the ruling?

Tom is allowed to redrop the ball (Decision 25-1b/6). If it rolls to deeper water again, he is allowed to place the ball where it first struck the bunker when redropped.

Change of Heart

What happens if a player lifts his ball, then decides not to take relief?

Brian elects to take relief from casual water and picks up his ball. He then realizes that the only area in which he may drop under the Rules is in the bushes where his ball, when dropped, will almost certainly be unplayable. Since the ball was playable in its original spot in the casual water, Brian replaces it and plays from there. What is the ruling?

Brian is penalized one stroke for lifting his ball in play (Rule 18-2a). He was entitled to lift his ball to take relief from casual water, but his right was negated when he elected not to take relief.

In taking relief from an abnormal ground condition, such as casual water, or an immovable obstruction, such as a cart path, Rule 25-1b provides for relief within one club-length of the point nearest to where the ball lies which is not nearer the hole, avoids interference with the condition, and is not in a hazard or on a green. This specific point can sometimes be in an unfriendly area, so it is best to weigh all options before picking up your ball. You might find you are better off playing it as it lies.

Now What If?

Brian's ball is unplayable in casual water. He announces that he will take relief for casual water, lifts his ball, then discovers that dropping within one club-length of the nearest point of relief will leave him with an unplayable lie. Using the original spot of the ball as a reference point will give him a better position under the unplayable ball Rule than the casual-water drop area. Can he declare the ball unplayable and use the original spot as the reference point?

If Brian uses the original spot as a reference point under Rule 28 (ball unplayable), he must suffer a one-stroke penalty for lifting his ball in play in addition to the one-stroke penalty for an unplayable ball. The additional penalty applies because he didn't declare the ball unplayable before lifting it.

All Wet

Does a player need to retrieve his ball from casual water to get relief?

Rich hits his tee shot into the fairway, but it ends up in a large puddle of casual water. He can see a ball toward the middle of the puddle, but he can't retrieve or identify it as his without sloshing through some ankle-deep water. Is he allowed to take relief?

Yes. A player is not obliged to use unreasonable effort to retrieve and identify a ball he sees in casual water, so long as there is reasonable evidence that his ball is in the casual water. Examples of sufficient evidence would be seeing the ball go into the water or the fact that the ball could easily be found if it were in the area near the casual water.

A different reference point for the drop is used if the ball is found or if it is lost in casual water (Rule 25-1). If the ball is

found, the player determines the nearest point of relief relative to the position of the ball, and drops within one club-length of that point. If the ball is lost, he uses the spot the ball last entered the casual water as his reference point. So, if a player can retrieve his ball from casual water without unreasonable effort, he must do so.

Now What If?

Rich hits his tee shot into the rough in an area he can't see from the tee. It turns out there is a large puddle of casual water in that area. He can see a ball toward the middle of the puddle, but it would be difficult to retrieve. Is he allowed to take relief from casual water?

Rich is not allowed relief from casual water without identifying the ball as his because there is not reasonable evidence that the ball is in the casual water; it might be lost in the nearby rough. In this case, he probably will want to get his feet wet to retrieve the ball to see if it is his; otherwise, he will have to take a stroke-and-distance penalty for a lost ball.

Burrowed Time

Relief from a burrowing animal hole can be very rewarding

Ed's tee shot comes to rest beneath a pine tree. From where his ball lies, his swing would be restricted by branches and he would have to chip sideways into the fairway. But it happens that the ball lies in a gopher hole, so Ed takes free relief from a hole made by a burrowing animal as allowed by the Rules. In doing so, Ed gets out from underneath the tree and is able to take a full swing and hit directly toward the green. Has Ed made a proper drop?

Yes, this procedure is entirely within the Rules. A player gets a free drop when a hole, cast, or runway made by a burrowing animal interferes with his stance or swing (Rule 25-1). The relief doesn't apply if it would be unreasonable for him to swing at the ball because of interference from something else, such as a tree or bush. In this case, however, Ed clearly would be able to take a swing, albeit a restricted one, so he's entitled to relief.

The relief point is the nearest point that avoids interference from the condition, is no nearer the hole, and is not in a hazard or on a putting green. The player takes a free drop within one club-length of this point. If this gets Ed out from under a tree, with a clear shot at the green, that's his good fortune. Any other considerations, such as going from a half swing to a full swing or obtaining a clearer line of play (or the reverse) are moot. Ed is simply lucky he found a well-placed gopher hole.

Now What If?

Ed's ball is just behind a tree and just in front of a cast made by a burrowing animal. The cast would not interfere with a sideways stroke back into the fairway, which is his only reasonable shot, but it would interfere with a stroke directly into the tree. May Ed claim he's going to play toward the green and take relief from the burrowing animal cast, thereby moving his ball from behind the tree?

No. A player does not get relief from a burrowing animal hole or cast if interference would occur only through the use of an unnecessarily abnormal stance, swing, or direction of play.

Stuck in a Rut

Is a player entitled to relief from a tire track?

Andy's ball comes to rest in a tire track made by a golf cart. The ground is soft, but the area is not considered to be casual water because no water is visible when Andy takes his stance. The track interferes with Andy's swing. Does he get relief?

It's a judgment call. The tire track could be considered ground under repair, from which Andy would get free relief, but that's up to the committee to decide (Rule 25).

In a tournament, the committee generally marks the areas of ground under repair with white lines. But if a player's ball ends up in an area he thinks is ground under repair, he can call in a member of the committee to make the determination. It is possible that the committee missed a spot, or that the damage occurred after the course was marked.

Decision 25/16 offers some guidance, but there are no hard-and-fast guidelines for relief from a tire track. The decision says that a "deep rut" is ground under repair, but not a "shallow indentation." The general principle involved in making the call is fairness to all competitors. If the track is deep enough that playing out of it clearly puts a player at a disadvantage against the rest of the field, it should be declared ground under repair.

Now What If?

Andy's ball is run over by a golf cart driven by a greenkeeper, causing the ball to become partially embedded in soft ground. What is the ruling?

This is a case of a ball at rest being moved (Rule 18), because the ball moved downward from its original position. There is no penalty, and Andy replaces the ball. Since the original lie was altered, he places the ball within one club-length in the nearest similar lie (Rule 20-3b).

CHAPTER NINE

Rules of Order

Who's Away?

How to determine the order of play when two balls
lie in the water

*Tom and Jeff both hit their balls into a lateral water hazard. Both balls
are visible, and Tom's is farther from the hole. Jeff's ball crossed the hazard line farther from the hole, so his drop is likely to leave him with the
longer shot. Both players decide to take relief. Who should play first?*

Tom should play first because his ball lies farther from the hole (Decision
10/2). The order of play is determined by the balls' positions on the course
before relief is taken. This applies if both players are taking relief under any
Rule, such as ground under repair. Also, if a player is taking a drop well

behind where his ball lies (as is quite possible under the water hazard and unplayable ball Rules), he should play after any other player whose ball lies farther from the hole than his original position.

We say "should" rather than "must" in these situations because there is no penalty for playing out of turn in stroke play, unless the players agree to do it to give one of them an advantage. However, if a player plays out of turn in match play, his opponent may require him to cancel the stroke and replay it, in correct order, without penalty.

Now What If?

Tom and Jeff both hit their balls in the same general area of a lateral water hazard. Both balls are lost in the hazard, so the players don't know which ball is farther from the hole. Jeff's ball crossed the hazard line farther from the hole. Who should play first?

The ball to be played first should be decided by lot (Decision 10/3). This is the same procedure followed when the balls are equidistant from the hole (Rule 10-1b and Rule 10-2b).

While You Wait

Is a trip to the practice green between nines allowed?

After his group completes the front nine, Craig sees there is a delay on the 10th tee. While waiting, he goes to the practice green and hits some putts. He is on the 10th tee by the time the group ahead has cleared. Is he penalized for practicing during a round?

There is no penalty. Between the play of two holes, a player is allowed to practice putting or chipping on or near the green of the hole last played, the teeing ground of the next hole, or any practice green, provided that the practice does not unduly delay play (Rule 7-2). That is the only practice allowed during a round: Any other practice strokes incur a two-stroke penalty in stroke play or loss of hole in match play.

This situation actually happened during the Doral-Ryder Open on the PGA Tour a few years ago (the player was Hubert Green). Tour officials were initially unsure of the ruling because the Tour adopts a Local Rule which further restricts practice between holes. But the Local Rule prohibits practice only on the green of the hole last played—practice putting or chipping on the practice green or the next tee is still allowed.

Incidentally, the USGA does not adopt the Local Rule in its events, which means that a player is allowed to practice putting on the green just finished—if the next group isn't waiting in the fairway.

Now What If?

After his group completes the front nine, Craig sees there is a delay on the 10th tee. He goes to the practice range and hits a few shots. Is he penalized for practicing during the round?

Yes. Only practice putting or chipping is allowed between holes. Hitting full shots on the range—or anywhere else—is prohibited. The penalty is two strokes in stroke play or loss of hole in match play, applied to the next hole.

Out of Range

Does hitting a range ball back where it belongs draw a penalty?

Steve is approaching his ball on the 10th fairway when he sees a practice ball from the adjacent practice range lying nearby. He hits the range ball back to the range, taking a full swing. Is he penalized for practicing during the round?

Yes. A player is not allowed to play a practice stroke during a round, with the exception of practice putting or chipping between the play of two holes (Rule 7-2). Steve is penalized two strokes in stroke play or loss of hole in match play.

If Steve had casually flicked the ball back to the range with his club, apparently only for the reason of tidying up the course, he would not have been penalized (Decision 7-2/5). But taking a normal stance and full swing at a range ball during a round is considered a practice stroke, no matter what the intent. A player also could be penalized for chipping the ball back to the range if he does it purposefully rather than casually—practice chipping is allowed only between the play of two holes.

The same general principle applies if a player finds an abandoned ball and hits it off the course, into a water hazard, back to his cart, etc. If he casually knocks it away there is no penalty, but a "normal" swing is considered practice.

Now What If?

While playing the 10th hole, Steve finds a plugged ball that was lost by Bill, who is in another group playing the adjacent 11th hole. When the ball is found, Bill is already walking up the 11th. After Steve calls to him, Bill requests the ball be returned to him. Bill is out of throwing range, so Steve hits the ball to him with a short iron. Is Steve penalized for practicing during a round?

No. Since Steve was acting out of courtesy, there's no penalty (Decision 7-2/5.5).

Calling Time-Out

When is a player allowed to discontinue play?

On his way from the 11th green to the 12th tee, Todd is stung by a bee. The sting is painful, and Todd is unable to continue play right away. He summons an official and asks for time to recover before resuming play. Should the official grant his request?

Yes, if Todd will be able to resume play within 15 minutes or so (Decision 6-8a/3). There are three situations, other than a suspension of play by the

Committee, when a player may discontinue play: If he believes there is danger from lightning, if he is seeking a decision from the committee on a doubtful or disputed point, or if there is some other good reason, such as sudden illness. Bad weather is not itself considered a valid reason.

A bee sting, heat exhaustion, or being struck by a golf ball are examples of "some other good reason." It is the player's responsibility to report to the committee as soon as possible upon discontinuing play. If his reason for stopping is satisfactory, there is no penalty. In cases of injury or sudden illness, the USGA says 15 minutes should be the maximum.

If a player discontinues play without reporting to the committee or if his reason for stopping is ruled unsatisfactory, the player is disqualified. In match play, however, if both players agree to discontinue play, they are not disqualified unless by doing so the competition is delayed.

Now What If?

Todd and Terry are playing in a stroke-play tournament. Between the 11th tee and 12th green, their golf cart breaks down. They discontinue play and return to the clubhouse to get another cart. Should they be penalized for discontinuing play?

No, they should not be penalized. The USGA, in Decision 6-8a/4, says that since it may not always be reasonable to expect players to carry their own bags, the Committee may consider the reason for discontinuance satisfactory. There is no penalty, provided that the players reported the problem promptly and resumed play when directed.

Checking It Out

Can a player practice putting on the course before a round?

Bill notices that the grass on the practice putting green hasn't been cut, so before his round he practices putting on the 18th green to get a better feel for the speed. Is this allowed?

Practicing on the course before a round is allowed only in match play. In stroke play, a competitor is not allowed to practice on the course or test the putting surface of any green before the round (Rule 7-1). In a stroke play competition, Bill would be disqualified.

This applies not only to practice putting. It is also prohibited in stroke play to hit practice balls off the first tee. The penalty is disqualification, though Decision 7-1b/1 allows a modification of the penalty to two strokes if a player hits only one ball off the tee into an adjacent area. The one exception allows a player to practice putting or chipping on or near the first tee before starting the round.

Bill would also be disqualified in stroke play for practicing on one of the course's greens before a playoff or between rounds of a tournament played on consecutive days at the same course.

The Rules note that it is permissible for the committee in charge of competition to either prohibit practice on the course in match play or allow it in stroke play. So, if the practice green is closed or a course has no practice green, the committee may allow pre-round putting practice on the course.

Now What If?

In stroke play, Bill's caddie practices on the 18th green before Bill starts the round. In view of the fact that a player is penalized for a breach of the Rules by his caddie, is Bill disqualified?

No. A player is responsible for his caddie's actions only during a round (Decision 7-1b/5). However, if the caddie was acting under the player's instructions, the Committee would be justified in disqualifying the player.

A Little Help

Can a player get a swing tip before a playoff?

Bill finishes a stroke play tournament tied for the lead, with other players still on the course. He goes to the range to hit practice balls in case he is in a playoff. While he is there, he asks for and receives advice from his teacher on his swing. Bill ends up in a sudden-death playoff. Is he penalized for asking for advice?

No. The prohibition against giving or asking for advice from anyone except a caddie, partner, or partner's caddie applies only during a stipulated round (Rule 8-1). The regulation 18 holes are considered to be the stipulated round. The playoff is a new round.

A player is also allowed to give advice to a fellow competitor between regulation play and a playoff. This happened at the 1997 Home Depot Invitational on the Senior PGA Tour. After Lee Trevino reached a playoff when Jim Dent missed a short putt on the 18th hole, Trevino advised Dent to take more time on important putts. Such a comment during the round would have drawn a two-stroke penalty for giving advice, which is defined as "any counsel or suggestion which could influence a player in determining his play, the choice of a club, or the method of making a stroke."

Trevino was involved in such a situation in the 1980 Tournament of Champions, though he was on the receiving end of the advice. During the round, fellow competitor Tom Watson told Trevino he was playing the ball too far forward in his stance. The remark was picked up by a television microphone, and Watson was slapped with a two-stroke penalty.

Now What If?

Bill is playing the sixth hole in a stroke play tournament when play is suspended. During the suspension, he seeks out his teacher for swing advice. Is Bill penalized?

No. The period when play is suspended is not "during the stipulated round," so Bill is allowed to ask for or give advice. He could also ask a fellow competitor for advice on club selection.

Bad Advice

A suggestion can be costly—for the person giving it

Tom hits his tee shot into the trees, with his ball coming to rest near a bush. His fellow competitor in stroke play, Paul, tells him, "It looks like you have no shot. If I were you, I would declare the ball unplayable." Is Paul in violation of the Rule on giving advice?

Yes. Paul is penalized two strokes for giving advice (Rule 8-1). Advice is defined as any counsel or suggestion that could influence a player in determining his play, the choice of a club, or the method of making a stroke. Paul's suggestion could influence Tom in determining his play, so it is a violation.

A player is allowed to give information on the Rules or on matters of public information, such as the location of hazards, the position of the flag-

stick on the green, or the yardage to the green from a fixed point. Paul would be allowed to explain the options under the unplayable ball Rule — that's information on the Rules — but he crosses the line by suggesting what Tom should do.

A player is also not allowed to *ask* for advice from anyone except his partner or caddie, so Tom would be penalized if he asked Paul whether he should take an unplayable lie, but not if he asked what his options were if he declared the ball unplayable. If Tom asks for advice and Paul responds by giving it, both are penalized.

Now What If?

Before playing his shot to the green, Paul asks a spectator to tell him how far Tom's ball, which is on the green, lies from the flagstick. Is Paul in violation of the Rule on asking for advice?

No. The position of Tom's ball on the green is considered public information, so the question is permissible even though the answer will help determine Paul's play.

Late Substitution

What happens if a player substitutes a ball during play of a hole to avoid confusion?

After playing their tee shots on a par-five hole, Dennis and Kevin realize that they are playing balls with identical markings. From watching their tee shots, they know which ball belongs to each of them, but to avoid possible confusion later on, Dennis lifts his ball and replaces it with a ball that has a different number. He plays out the hole with the substituted ball. Is this allowed?

N o. A player must hole out with the ball he played from the tee unless a Rule permits him to substitute another ball. Since no Rule allows for substitution in this case, Dennis is penalized. In match play, he loses the hole. In stroke play, he incurs a total penalty of three strokes—one stroke for lifting his ball in play (Rule 18-2a), and two strokes for substituting a ball (Rule 15-1). If he had realized his mistake before playing the substituted ball, he could have gone back to the original ball and been penalized only

one stroke (Rule 20-6). He also would have incurred a one-stroke penalty if he had lifted his original ball and put an identifying mark on it.

Dennis's actions are understandable in that both players would be forced to take a stroke-and-distance penalty for a lost ball if, later in the play of the hole, they can't identify which ball is which. But, the Rules-makers would say that's something they should have thought about before teeing off with identical balls.

Now What If?

Dennis marks the position of his ball on the green and lifts it. When he is ready to play, by mistake he replaces the original ball with another ball he was carrying in his pocket. He holes out with the substituted ball and tees off on the next hole before realizing his mistake. Is there a penalty?

Yes. In match play, he loses the hole for substituting a ball. In stroke play, he is penalized two strokes.

Pit Stop

Is a lunch stop allowed under the Rules?

Scott, Mark, John, and Chris are playing in a stroke play tournament at their club. After nine holes, they stop in the halfway house for refreshment and sit down for 10 minutes to eat. Is this allowed?

No. Rule 6-8a says that a player shall not discontinue play unless he believes there is danger from lightning, he is seeking a decision from the Committee on a doubtful or dubious point, the committee has suspended play, or there is some other good reason such as sudden illness. Stopping for lunch is not considered a good reason, and all four players are disqualified from the competition for not playing continuously.

This Rule does not prohibit a player from getting food from a halfway house, but he must proceed immediately to the next tee and eat while continuing his round. However, even in this quick stop, he must not unduly delay his own play, that of his opponent, or that of any other competitor. If he does, he is subject to a two-stroke (stroke play) or loss-of-hole (match play) penalty under Rule 6-7.

Decision 6-8a/2.5 says that a committee cannot under the Rules of Golf make a condition of competition that allows players to discontinue play for refreshment for an extended period. It may permit players to discontinue play for a short period of time (up to five minutes) if it considers there to be good reason, such as a danger of dehydration in hot weather.

Now What If?

Scott, Mark, John, and Chris are playing in a match play tournament. After nine holes, they stop in the halfway house for refreshment and sit down for 10 minutes to eat. Is this allowed?

Yes. Rule 6-8a includes an exception that says players discontinuing match play by agreement are not subject to disqualification unless by doing so the competition is delayed. So, if all players agree to stop for a bite to eat, there is no penalty.

Second Thoughts

Can a player pick up a second ball once he has put it in play?

Art is playing in a stroke-play tournament. His ball lies on a road, and he isn't sure if the road is an obstruction. He announces that he will play out the hole with two balls—the original and a second ball dropped under the obstruction Rule—and that he wishes the score with the second ball to count if the Rules permit. He hits his original ball onto the green and the second ball into a bunker. He picks up the second ball, holes out the original ball, and plays from the next tee. What is the ruling?

If the Committee rules that the road is an obstruction, the score with the second ball would have counted. However, since Art didn't hole out with that ball, he is disqualified. If the road isn't an obstruction, there is no penalty. In that case, a score with the second ball wouldn't have counted, and Art's score with the original ball is his score for the hole.

Rule 3-3 allows a player to play a second ball when he is in doubt as to procedure—but only in stroke play. He should announce which ball he wants to count if the Rules permit. If he makes a different score with the two balls, he must report the situation to the Committee before returning his scorecard. If he makes a higher score with the ball he selected in advance, and that procedure is allowed under the Rules, he must take that score. If he doesn't select a preferred ball in advance, the score with the original ball counts if it is played under an allowed procedure.

Now What If?

In stroke play, Art plays his original ball from a road. After hitting the shot, he realizes that the road might be an obstruction. He drops a second ball and says he wishes that ball to count under Rule 3-3. The road is indeed an obstruction. Which ball counts?

The original ball counts. Rule 3-3 can't be invoked after playing the original ball. The player must announce his intention when the situation arises, not after taking further action.

CHAPTER TEN

Equipment

Slippery When Wet

What is allowed to keep a wet grip from slipping in your hands?

Rick is playing in a steady rain. As he nears the end of the round, he has trouble keeping the grips of his clubs dry. On the 15th hole, Rick pulls out a handkerchief and wraps it around the grip of his club to help him hold on during his swing. Is this allowed?

Yes. Although Rule 14-3 prohibits the use of artificial devices or unusual equipment during a round, it lists as exceptions several things that are allowed to assist a player in gripping the club: 1) plain gloves may be worn; 2) resin, powder, and drying or moisturizing agents may be used; 3) tape or gauze may be applied to the grip (provided such application does not make the grip nonconforming); and 4) a towel or handkerchief may be wrapped about the grip.

    Any of these may be used during the course of a round without violating Rule 4-2, which prohibits changing the playing characteristics of a club.

It is also permissible to apply tape to a glove. If tape is applied to the grip of a club, the grip must remain conforming, that is, "straight and plain in form" and "not molded for any part of the hands."

No, unless Rick started with less than the maximum of 14 clubs. He is allowed to replace a club if it becomes "unfit for play," but a slippery grip doesn't qualify (Decision 4-4a/1). If he carries the extra driver, the penalty is two strokes per hole in stroke play, with a maximum of four strokes. In match play, the state of the match is adjusted by deducting one hole for each hole a breach occurred, with a maximum deduction of two holes.

Damaged Goods?

Declaring a ball unfit for play requires a specific procedure

John catches his approach shot thin, but it ends up on the green. He marks his ball, inspects it, and throws it into an adjacent lake from which it cannot be retrieved. He then says that the ball was damaged and unfit for play, and that he is substituting another ball. He did not announce his intentions in advance, nor did he give his fellow competitor or opponent a chance to examine the ball. What is the ruling?

John incurs a penalty of loss of hole in match play or two strokes in stroke play. He may substitute another ball to finish the hole.

A ball is unfit for play only if it is visibly cut, cracked, or out of shape — a scratched or scraped surface or damage to the paint is not sufficient (Rule 5-3). If a player thinks his ball has become unfit for play during play of a hole, he may lift his ball. He must announce his intentions beforehand, then give his fellow competitor in stroke play or opponent in match play a chance to examine the ball. If it is unfit for play, he may substitute another ball. If not, he replaces the original.

The provision that another player must examine the ball prevents the Rule from being abused. In this case, because the ball is irretrievable, John

incurs the general two-stroke or loss-of-hole penalty under Rule 5-3 (or the same penalty for playing a wrong ball, but only one is applied).

Now What If?

After hitting his tee shot, John says he thinks the ball behaved erratically in flight. Before hitting his next shot, he examines the ball but finds no external damage and the ball is not out of shape. He says the ball must have been damaged internally when it was hit off the tee and says the ball is unfit for play. Is he allowed to substitute another ball?

No. A ball is unfit for play only if it is visibly cut, cracked, or out of shape. John may not substitute another ball until he finishes the hole (Decision 5-3/1).

Weighty Issue

Is a player allowed to take a training aid onto the course?

While waiting to play from the eighth tee, Scott swings a club with a weighted "donut," a training aid used to make the club heavier for practice swings. When it is his turn to play, he removes the donut and hits his tee shot. Is this allowed?

No. The use of this, or any device designed as a training or swing aid, is prohibited during a round. The penalty is severe: disqualification in either match play or stroke play. Such training aids fall under the category "artificial devices and unusual equipment."

Rule 14-3 bans such equipment during a round if it might assist the player in making a stroke or in his play, if it is used for the purpose of gauging or measuring distance or conditions which might affect his play, or if it might assist him in gripping the club (with certain exceptions). Swinging a club with a weighted donut might assist the player in making a subsequent stroke, so it is prohibited. Also prohibited are any of a number of swing aids, such as straps designed to help the player keep his arms or body in the proper position. These are to be used on the practice range only, with one exception: A player can use a donut or other device for practice swings on the first tee as long as he removes it before making his first stroke. Using the device is not allowed "during" a round, and the round doesn't start until the player makes his first stroke.

Now What If?

Scott carries a heavy training club in his bag and uses it during a round for practice swings before hitting tee shots with his regular driver. Is this allowed?

Yes, but only if the weighted club doesn't put him over the 14-club limit. The Rules do not regulate the weight of clubs, so if the weighted club otherwise conforms with the Rules, the player is allowed to select it as one of his 14 clubs.

"X" Marks the Spot

Is an "X-out" ball allowed in competition?

While competing in his club championship, Andrew uses an "X-out" golf ball, a ball that the manufacturer considers to be imperfect and sells with the brand name crossed out. His fellow competitor, Tony, questions whether or not it is legal to use the ball. Is the use of an X-out ball permitted by the Rules?

Generally, the use of an X-out ball is permitted. Decision 5-1/4 reasons that the majority of X-out balls are rejected only for aesthetic reasons, such as an imperfect paint job, so the ball is allowed unless there is strong evidence to suggest that it doesn't conform to the Rules. The ball would be illegal if it were heavier than 1.62 ounces, smaller than 1.68 inches in diameter, or if there were strong evidence that it didn't meet the spherical symmetry standard (for example, a ball designed to self-correct in flight) or initial velocity standard (a "hot" ball).

The use of an X-out ball is not permitted if the committee running the competition has adopted the condition that the player must use a ball that is named on the List of Conforming Golf Balls published by the USGA, even if the ball in question (without the X's) does appear on the List.

Now What If?

The committee has adopted the condition of competition that players must use a brand of ball on the current List of Conforming Golf Balls. The USGA recommends a penalty of disqualification if a committee sets such a condition. Does the USGA allow the committee to stipulate that the penalty for using a ball not on the List is loss of hole in match play or two strokes in stroke play for each hole at which a breach occurs?

Yes. However, if the ball obviously does not meet the prescribed specifications, such as for size and weight, the player is disqualified.

CHAPTER ELEVEN

Match Play

Pickup Game

Before conceding a putt—or picking up an opponent's marker—you'd better know the score

Greg and Jeff are playing a match. Greg holes a putt for a four and, thinking he has won the hole, picks up the coin marking the position of Jeff's ball. Actually, Jeff's putt is for a four. Is picking up the coin considered to have been a concession of Jeff's next stroke?

No, but the result is the same—the hole is halved. Picking up the coin is not in itself a concession unless the player also says, "This putt is good," or something to that effect. The penalty for picking up the coin is the same as the penalty for picking up an opponent's ball—one stroke (Rule 18-2b). However, according to Rule 2-2, once a player has holed out and his opponent is left with a stroke for the half, if the player thereafter incurs a penalty, the hole is halved. If Jeff had a putt to win the hole when Greg picked up his coin, Greg would be penalized one stroke and Jeff would now have two putts to win the hole. For example, Greg makes a six and picks up Jeff's coin thinking Jeff is putting for a four when actually the putt is for a five. With the penalty, Greg's score becomes a seven and Jeff has two putts to win.

Greg isn't any better off if he verbally concedes Jeff's putt. Once he grants the concession, Greg can't withdraw it (unless his mistake is due to Jeff giving him wrong information, in which case Jeff loses the hole).

Now What If?

Before a match, Greg and Jeff agree to concede all putts "inside the leather." Is this allowed?

No. Players can only concede the "next stroke" to an opponent (Rule 2-4); they can not agree in advance to concede putts within a specified length. Therefore, Greg and Jeff have agreed to waive Rule 1-1, which says that the game of golf consists of playing the ball into the hole, and both are disqualified under Rule 1-3.

Judge and Jury

Can a player choose to ignore a penalty committed by his match-play opponent?

Craig and Sam are playing a match. On the 12th hole, Craig sees Sam pick up a pine cone that lies near his ball in a bunker. Sam is unaware he has committed an infraction, but Craig knows it's against the Rules to remove loose impediments in a hazard. Is Craig obligated to call the penalty?

No. It is up to the player whether or not to make a claim in match play (Decision 2-5/1). In stroke play, it would be Craig's duty to call the penalty to protect the rest of the field.

There is an obligation in match play on the player who commits an infraction to inform his opponent of the penalty. If he doesn't do so promptly, he is deemed to have given wrong information about strokes taken even if he was unaware of the violation (Rule 9-2). In this case, Sam doesn't realize he's broken a Rule. He is subject to a loss-of-hole penalty both for removing the pinecone and for giving wrong information. But if Craig doesn't make a claim, there is no penalty. Craig might keep quiet because he doesn't want to win the hole on what he considers a silly penalty, or perhaps he doesn't want to call a penalty on a friend.

However, if Sam informs Craig of the penalty, Craig is not allowed to refuse it. This would be considered an agreement to waive the Rules, for which both players are subject to disqualification (Rule 1-3).

Now What If?

Craig and Sam are playing a match. On the 12th hole, Craig sees Sam pick up a pinecone that lies near his ball in a bunker. Sam is unaware he has committed an infraction. Craig doesn't say anything at the time, but after finishing play on the 18th with the match even he claims the match because of Sam's violation on the 12th. Is this allowed?

No. Any claim in match play must be made before teeing off on the next hole or leaving the green on the last hole of the match. No later claim can be considered unless it is based on facts previously unknown to the player making the claim and the player had been given wrong information. In this case, the facts were previously known to Craig. If Craig had not seen the violation, and was told about it by someone else when he came off the 18th green, the claim would be valid (Rule 2-5) if the result of the match hadn't been officially announced.

Know Your Strokes

It's up to the player to be aware of where handicap strokes fall

Al and Bob are playing a match. On the fourth tee, Al states that he gets a handicap stroke on the hole. When the players reach the green, Bob checks the scorecard and notices that Al shouldn't receive a stroke. Bob, saying he would have played the hole differently had he known there was no stroke given, claims the hole based on Al giving wrong information. What is the ruling?

There is no penalty, and the players should complete the hole without a stroke being given to Al.

Each player is responsible for knowing the holes at which handicap strokes are to be given or received once the players have declared their handicaps at the start of the match (Rule 6-2). Since both players have correctly stated their handicaps, Al's mistake in announcing that he gets a stroke on the hole does not constitute wrong information. The loss-of-hole penalty for wrong information concerns only information about strokes taken (Rule 9-2).

If the players don't discover until after finishing the fourth hole that no stroke should have been given, they still can make the correction before teeing off on the next hole simply by taking away the handicap stroke and adjusting the result. But once they start the fifth hole, the result of the fourth hole stands as played, even if it is later discovered that no stroke should have been given (Rule 2-5).

Al announces on the fourth tee that he gets a stroke. He makes a four on the hole. Bob, with a putt for a four, concedes the hole to Al and picks up. Before either player tees off on the next hole, Bob checks the scorecard and sees that Al shouldn't have received a stroke. What is the ruling?

The result stands. Al won the hole when Bob conceded it, and a concession can't be withdrawn (Rule 2-4). It is Bob's responsibility to know where the handicap strokes fall. However, if Bob had not said anything about conceding the hole and had made his putt for a four, the hole would be halved.

Taking It Back

Can a concession of a putt be withdrawn?

*In match play, Jeff finishes the hole with a six and concedes his oppo-
nent, Patrick, a four-foot putt, thinking that Patrick has two putts to
win the hole with a five. Jeff then realizes that Patrick actually was
lying four and needed to make the four-footer to win the hole. Can Jeff
withdraw his concession and ask Patrick to putt?*

No. Concession of a stroke, hole, or match may not be withdrawn once it is given (Rule 2-4). The putt is good as soon as Jeff concedes it, so

Patrick wins the hole even if he hasn't yet picked up the ball when Jeff changes his mind. The only exception would be if Jeff's mistake about how many strokes Patrick had taken were caused by wrong information given by Patrick, such as failing to inform Jeff of a penalty stroke, in which case Patrick would lose the hole (Rule 9-2).

Patrick is not allowed to decline the concession, even if he wants to as a sporting gesture. If he insists on putting, and misses, he still wins the hole because the hole was completed when Jeff conceded the putt.

If Jeff had picked up Patrick's ball or ball marker without verbally conceding the stroke, he would not have been deemed to have conceded the putt. However, he would be assessed a one-stroke penalty, so Patrick now would have two putts to win the hole after replacing his ball.

Now What If?

In a match between Jeff and Patrick, Jeff makes a statement which Patrick interprets to mean that his next putt is conceded. Patrick lifts his ball, but Jeff then says that he did not concede the putt. What is the ruling?

If Jeff's statement could reasonably have led Patrick to believe his next putt was conceded, Patrick should replace his ball without penalty. Otherwise, Patrick incurs a one-stroke penalty for lifting his ball without marking its position and replaces his ball (Decision 2-4/3).

Late Discovery

What happens if a violation is discovered after the end of a match?

Nick wins his match against Brian by a 3 and 2 margin. The two continue their rounds and while they are in the 18th fairway, Brian discovers that Nick has 15 clubs in his bag. Does Brian have a valid claim against Nick for violating the 14-club Rule or is it too late because the match is over?

Brian has a valid claim. Nick incurs the penalty for playing with more than 14 clubs for two or more holes, which is that two holes are deducted from the state of the match when the breach is discovered (Rule 4-4). The players must return to the 17th tee and resume the match, with Nick holding a 1-up lead.

Generally, in match play a player must make a claim before any player in the match plays from the next tee or before the players leave the last green of the match (Rule 2-5). A later claim is considered if it is based on facts previously unknown to the player making the claim and the player had been given wrong information by his opponent. Failing to report penalty strokes is considered giving wrong information even if the player is unaware of the penalty. However, once the result of the match has been officially announced—not the case in this example—no claim is considered unless the offending player *knowingly* gave wrong information.

Now What If?

Nick wins his match against Brian by a 2-up margin. Before the result is officially announced, Brian reports to the committee that he noticed on the 10th hole that Nick had 15 clubs in his bag, but didn't say anything at the time. What is the ruling?

The result of the match stands. Since Brian saw the violation on the 10th hole, his claim would have been valid only if he made it before either player teed off on the 11th hole.

State of Confusion

What happens when players are mistaken about the status of a match?

In a match-play event at their club, Craig and Mark leave the 18th green thinking their match is all square. They play extra holes and Mark wins at the 20th hole. Then, Craig and Mark both realize that Craig was actually one up after 18 holes. Who is declared the winner of the match?

Mark is the winner. In match play, if there is a doubt or dispute between the players, any claim must be made before either player tees off on the next hole (Rule 2-5). No later claim can be made unless it is based on facts previously unknown to the player making the claim, and he was given wrong information by his opponent on the number of strokes taken on a hole. Since that isn't the case here—the players were just mistaken—the match must be considered all square as soon as either player hits from the 19th tee. Similarly, if Craig and Mark were all square after 18 but mistakenly reported a one-up win for Mark, the win for Mark would stand if no wrong information had been given.

Such confusion can arise in match play because there is no official scorecard to turn in at the end of the match (Rule 6-6 on scoring applies only to stroke play). The players need report only the result, not their hole-by-hole scores. Of course, it is a good idea for each player to keep a score-card in case a dispute arises.

Now What If?

When they leave the 18th green of their match, Mark claims he is one up, while Craig claims the match is all square. The tournament committee gathers all available evidence, but is unable to determine the true state of the match. What should the committee do?

Decision 34-3/5 states the committee "should resolve the matter in the fairest way," and goes on to suggest that an equitable solution would be to order that the match be replayed.

Information Please

How quickly do you need to tell your opponent you've incurred a penalty?

Jim is hitting an iron shot from an uphill lie. After he addresses the ball and starts his backswing, the ball moves. He continues his swing and hits the ball, which ends up near the green. Under Rule 18-2, Jim incurs a one-stroke penalty. Jim's match-play opponent, Harry, then hits his second shot. As the two players approach the vicinity of the green, Jim informs Harry that he incurred a penalty stroke, so that he lies three instead of two. Has Jim acted properly?

No. Rule 9-2 states that a player who has incurred a penalty shall inform his opponent as soon as practicable, unless he is obviously proceeding under a Rule involving a penalty and this has been observed by his opponent. Since the penalty wasn't obvious, and Jim waited to inform Harry, Jim is deemed to be guilty of giving wrong information during the play of a hole, and he loses the hole.

The idea behind the Rule is that a player's strategy and play could be affected by wrong information. Harry, for example, might have played a safe

shot to the center of the green if he'd known Jim was lying three. Generally, a player should inform his opponent before the opponent plays his next stroke, but the phrase "as soon as practicable" absolves a player if his opponent is far away and plays quickly. This penalty applies only in match play. In stroke play, there is no penalty.

Now What If?

Jim's ball moves after he addresses it and begins his backswing. He hits the ball and, not knowing the Rule, is unaware that he has incurred a penalty. His opponent, Harry, then plays his next shot. As the two are walking to the green, Jim tells Harry that his ball moved as he was swinging at it. What is the ruling?

Jim loses the hole for not informing Harry of the penalty as soon as practicable. The fact that he was unaware of the penalty doesn't matter.

CHAPTER TWELVE

Four-Ball/ Foursomes Play

Team Concept

Is a player penalized for his partner's actions?

Al and Bob are playing Charlie and Don in four-ball match play. Al, who has a 10-foot putt for a half, taps down a spike mark on his line. Charlie calls Al's infraction, which carries a loss-of-hole penalty. Bob has a six-foot putt for a half, but Charlie claims the team loses the hole because of Al's penalty. Bob says he should still be alive for the hole. Who is right?

Bob is correct. In a team match, a penalty (one or two strokes or loss of hole) applies to a player's partner only if the infraction assists the partner's play or adversely affects an opponent's play. Neither is the case here.

When the penalty is loss of hole and doesn't apply to the partner, the guilty player is disqualified for the hole, but his partner can still win or halve the hole for the team (Rule 30-3f). In four-ball stroke play, if a player's breach assists his partner, the partner incurs the applicable stroke penalty (Rule 31-8).

Other provisions of Rule 30-3 specify that the side shall be penalized if either player breaches the 14-club rule, that a partner incurs no penalty for a wrong ball even if it is his ball that is played, and that the side is disqualified from the match for breaches by either partner carrying that penalty except for time of starting and discontinuance of play.

Now What If?

In a four-ball match, Bob has a six-foot putt for par. His partner, Al, taps down a spike mark on Bob's line. What is the penalty?

Al and Bob lose the hole. Al is penalized for a breach of Rule 16-1 (touching the line of putt). Since his partner was assisted by the breach, Bob suffers the same loss-of-hole penalty.

Alternate Question

What do you do when a tee shot heads out of bounds in foursomes play?

Tom and Mark are playing in a foursomes (alternate-shot) competition. Tom hits his drive and thinks his ball might be out of bounds. They decide to play a provisional ball. Who plays it, Tom or Mark?

Mark plays the provisional ball, because if the original ball is indeed out of bounds (or lost), it would be his turn to play (Decision 29-1/3). If the original ball is found in bounds, the provisional ball is picked up, and Mark takes his normal turn by hitting the second shot with the original.

If Tom plays the provisional ball when Mark should have, there is no penalty if the original ball is found in bounds and the provisional ball doesn't become the ball in play. But if the original ball is out of bounds (or lost), Mark and Tom lose the hole in match play for playing in the incorrect order. In stroke play, they incur a two-stroke penalty, the provisional ball is abandoned, and Mark must play from the tee (hitting five — stroke-and-distance plus the two-stroke penalty). If they don't correct the error before playing from the next tee, or leaving the green if it's the last hole, they are disqualified.

It should also be noted that in an alternate-shot format, penalty strokes don't affect the order of play. So, in the case of a one-stroke penalty after the tee shot, the player who hit the first stroke would then hit the fourth stroke.

Now What If?

Tom and Mary are playing in a mixed-foursome (alternate-shot) competition, where the men play from the men's tees and the women from the women's tees. Tom hits his tee shot out of bounds. Does Mary play the next stroke from the women's tee or the men's tee?

Mary must play from the men's tee (Decision 29/2). The fact that she plays from the women's tee on the holes where she hits the first stroke doesn't enable her to move up when the ball has been put in play from the men's tee.

Hands-on Procedure

Can a player line up his partner's putter?

Keith and Bill are partners in a team match. Bill has been having trouble with his aim, so before he hits a putt, Keith physically aligns Bill's putter so that it is aimed on the proper line. Keith moves away before the stroke. Is this allowed?

Yes. Although Rule 14-2 says that a player is not allowed to accept physical assistance or protection from the elements in making a stroke, it does not apply prior to the stroke. This means that a player can have someone physically help him align his body or club before the stroke. It also means that a caddie or partner can hold an umbrella over a player's head before, but not during, the stroke.

There is a further prohibition on the green, where a player is not allowed to let his caddie, partner, or partner's caddie position himself behind the ball on the line of the putt, but again this applies only during the stroke (Rule 16-1f). Sometimes on the pro Tours, you will see a player have his caddie stand behind him before the stroke to help with alignment, and then move away before the stroke. So far, to our knowledge, none of them have resorted to receiving physical assistance, though it is allowed by

the Rules. Anywhere except the green, a caddie or partner may stand on the line of play behind the ball even during a stroke.

Now What If?

Keith and Bill are partners in a team match played late in the day. The sun is shining in Bill's eyes as he stands over a putt. Keith purposely stands between Bill and the setting sun to reduce the sun's glare while Bill hits the putt. Is this allowed?

No. This is considered to be accepting protection from the elements in making a stroke. The penalty is two strokes in stroke play or loss of hole in match play.

Something Borrowed

Todd and Joe are partners in a four-ball competition. Several times during the round, Todd, who is carrying only 13 clubs, borrows Joe's driver. Have Todd and Joe violated the 14-club Rule?

Yes. There is a provision that partners may share clubs (Rule 4-4b), but they may do so only if the total number carried by the partners is not more than 14. In other words, two or more players who are partners in a team match may share a single set of clubs, but if each is carrying anything close to a full set of clubs, they aren't allowed to share. This means that your partner's driver is off limits, even if you feel like you hit it better than your own. It also means that if you leave your putter in the cart, you can't borrow your partner's.

The penalty in stroke play is two strokes for each hole at which any breach occurred, with a maximum penalty per round of four strokes. In match play, at the conclusion of the hole at which the breach is discovered, the state of the match is adjusted by deducting one hole (for example, from 2 up to 1 up) if it occurred on only one hole, or deducting two holes if it occurred on two or more holes (whether the side won or lost the holes where a breach occurred is irrelevant). In team play, the side is penalized for a breach of the 14-club Rule by either player (Rule 30-3b).

Now What If?

Todd is playing in an individual competition. He discovers on one green that he left his putter on the previous green, and borrows a putter from his fellow competitor, Joe, to finish the hole. Todd is carrying 13 clubs. Is this allowed?

No. In individual competition, a player is not allowed to borrow another player's club, even if the player who is doing the borrowing has fewer than 14 clubs (Rule 4-4a). Todd is penalized two strokes in stroke play or the deduction of one hole in match play.

Late Arrival

Bill and Gary are playing a four-ball match against Tom and Alan. Gary is late, and Bill plays the first hole representing the side by himself, with his score counting against the better ball of the other two. Gary arrives after the other three players have hit their tee shots on the second hole. Gary then tees off and plays the second hole. Gary makes a par, while Bill, Tom, and Alan make bogeys. What is the ruling?

It is permissible for Bill to start the match without Gary. A four-ball side may be represented by one partner for all or any part of the match; all partners need not be present (Rule 30-3a). However, an absent partner may join a match only between holes, not during the play of a hole.

Since all three of the other players had teed off when he arrived, Gary joined the match during play of the second hole. He incurs the general match-play penalty of loss of hole, which in a team match means he is disqualified from the hole. The team halves the hole with Bill's bogey—unless any of Gary's strokes on the hole assisted Bill's play, in which case Bill is also disqualified from the hole and the side loses the hole.

The general principle in four-ball matches is if a player's breach of a Rule assists his partner's play or adversely affects an opponent's play, the partner incurs the applicable penalty in addition to the penalty incurred by the player (Rule 30-3f).

Now What If?

Gary is late for his four-ball match, arriving after the other three players have teed off on the second hole. He is not allowed to join the match until the third hole, but is he allowed to give his partner, Bill, advice during play of the second hole?

Yes. Although not allowed to play the second hole, Gary is free to give advice, such as on club selection or reading the green.

Getting the Line

Can a player stand behind the ball to look at the break of his partner's putt?

Sam and Dave are partners in a team match. On the first hole, Sam has a putt on the same line as Dave's. While Dave putts, Sam stands behind him on an extension of the line of the putt to get a better view of the break. Is this allowed?

No. Sam and Dave lose the hole in match play and each are penalized two strokes in stroke play. Dave is penalized under Rule 16-1f, which says that while making a stroke on the putting green the player shall not allow his caddie, his partner, or his partner's caddie to position himself on or close to an extension of the line of putt behind the ball. Sam is penalized under Rule 30-3f (match play) or Rule 31-8 (stroke play) because his play was assisted. However, if Sam does not have a putt on a similar line, only Dave is penalized.

Rule 16-1f entered the books in the 1970s to stop the practice of Tour caddies crouching behind players when they putted in order to help with alignment of the putter blade (they can still do so before the player putts). As a byproduct of the ban for caddies and partners, it also became illegal for a partner to get a view of the line by standing behind it while the player makes a stroke.

It doesn't matter that Sam's intention is to see the break and not to help Dave's alignment. But there is no penalty on either player if Sam absent-mindedly stands on an extension of the line behind the ball while not paying any attention to Dave's putt (Decision 16-1f2).

Now What If?

Dave is putting the ball from just off the green. His partner, Sam, stands behind him on an extension of the line of play to get a better view of the break. Is this allowed?

Yes. Rule 16-1f applies only when the player is making a stroke from the putting green. When the ball is off the green, his partner or caddie may stand behind him on the line of play.

Index